Excerpts from a new England

Excerpts from a new England

Gareth Southgate:
Eight years
and Eighteen
episodes

David Winner

Series curator Ian Ridley

First published by Pitch Publishing
and Floodlit Dreams, 2024

Floodlit Dreams

Pitch Publishing
9 Donnington Park, 85 Birdham Road,
Chichester, West Sussex, PO20 7AJ
www.pitchpublishing.co.uk
info@pitchpublishing.co.uk

A CIP catalogue record is available for this book
from the British Library.

ISBN 978-1-83680-016-3

Cover by Steve Leard
Typesetting and origination by Pitch Publishing

Printed and bound in the UK on FSC® certified paper in line
with our continuing commitment to ethical business practices,
sustainability and the environment.

Printed and bound by CPI Antony Rowe, UK

For Anthony Winner

(1932–2021)

Introduction

'TO BE sane in a world of madmen is in itself madness,' said Jean-Jacques Rousseau. But I'm trying to get at something else. 'In madness lies sanity,' said Alan Watts, to which I say: no, no, no, that's not it at all. And here's another one: 'I became insane with long intervals of horrible sanity.' Interesting from Edgar Allan Poe, but hardly the thing I seek.

I'm googling various combinations of the words 'madness', 'time' and 'sanity', hoping to find something deep and/or witty to capture the essence of my feelings about Gareth Southgate's time as England manager. It's not working. Maybe Dostoyevsky had a cracking, quotable line? Or *The Simpsons*? But I'll try to say it in my own feeble way.

Perhaps I'll even write a little book exploring the subject.

Here's what it is. I reckon the key to Gareth's time as manager of the senior England men's team lies in some hitherto unexplored combination of the three words. He's a sane man in a time of madness. I began to think about this when I looked up the newspapers for the day of his first game in charge. It was against Malta on 8 October 2016: a routine World Cup qualifier against limited opponents and England won 2-0. Like any game of football, it would have held a variety of meanings, some deep, some trivial, some great, some small for those who took part, attended or watched on a screen. It is unlikely to resonate down the ages.

Elsewhere, though, something highly resonant happened. In America the day before the Malta game, news broke that the Republican candidate for the US presidency, Donald Trump, had been caught on tape some years earlier saying something vile about women: 'I don't even wait. And when you're a star, they let you do it. You can do anything. ... Grab 'em by the pussy. You can do anything.' With just a month to go before the election, that should have been the end of his candidacy. But he brazened it out, dismissed the recording as 'locker room talk', survived and won the election. The madness has not stopped since.

As I write, barely two months before the 2024 US election, Trump stands as an adjudicated rapist, convicted felon, and out-and-out racist and fascist who's made no secret of his desire, among other things, to tear down the US Constitution, rule as a dictator, inflict cruelties and deportation on millions of immigrants and smash environmental protections. He is said to be close to winning again. Britain's own era of madness had started slightly earlier, with the Brexit referendum, which was followed in football, four days later, by England's defeat by Iceland. The streams began to cross. Manager Roy Hodgson left, soon replaced by Sam Allardyce, who didn't last long, and, in politics, Britain began to resemble an Untied Kingdom. Over the next eight years there was plenty of craziness elsewhere, too: Covid, the Ukraine war, the roiling horrors of the Middle East, accelerating climate peril. You don't need the list.

And somehow, in the middle of all this madness, a sane and decent figure emerged in charge of an important national institution. As England manager between 2016 and 2024, Gareth Southgate seemed to transcend his sport and became something of a counterbalancing presence in a turbulent time.

There's been plenty of good journalism about Gareth's time as England boss (and much bad journalism), and two central works so far, both named *Dear England*. James Graham's hit stage play, and Rob Draper and Jonathan Northcroft's excellent, detailed account of his years up to the eve of the 2024 Euros, both took their title from the great open letter Gareth wrote to the nation in 2021. Very loosely based on the Taoist idea that all things are connected to all other things, I've tried to create something else: a collage of eighteen episodes over Gareth's eight years, mixed with other subjects, and with news cuttings to capture something of the spirit of Gareth and his time.

I hope it resonates, because it's been our time, too.

1
Our Iceland Story: The First Four Minutes

European Championship Round of 16: Nice, France, 27 June 2016

AS A child I loved the stories in Henrietta Elizabeth Marshall's classic *Our Island Story*. Brave Boadicea! Plucky Plantagenets! Princes in the Tower! Drake calmly playing bowls before whumping the Armada. Walter Raleigh laying down his cape for Good Queen Bess. Noble Lord Nelson telling his men 'England expects' before Trafalgar.

It never occurred to me that the stories might not be entirely true or could be construed as ever so slightly propagandist. I accepted without question that I was part of an ancient people who lived on a 'little green island set in the lonely sea'. It took me decades to clock that I might not be related to Hengist and Horsa.

In Marshall's telling, some English kings and queens may have been weak or wicked, others wise and excellent, but the people were righteous and endlessly good-hearted. For millennia they had resisted European tyrants such as Julius Caesar, Philip of Spain and Napoleon. Marshall's explanation of empire sounded good too:

> The people of Britain … grew to be a great people, till the little green island set in the lonely sea was no longer large enough to contain them all. Then they sailed away over the blue waves to far-distant countries. Now the people of the little island possess lands all over the world. These lands form the empire of Greater Britain. Many of these lands are far, far larger than the little island itself. Yet the people who live in them still look back lovingly to the little island, from which they or their fathers came, and call it 'Home'.

No proper modern historian would accept this guff for half a millisecond, yet as *The Times* put it, for fifty years this was the standard and much-loved book by which children learned the history of England.

And it leads us to Gareth Southgate's inheritance.

Looking again at my old hardback copy of *Our Island Story*, I notice the cover features the Three Lions badge, plus a crown and some leaves. And I can't help but notice the proto-Brexity language of some of the text. The long reign of Henry III, for instance, 'was not a happy one for England yet good came of it, for his very weakness made the people strong, and out of the troubles of his reign grew our freedom of speech and our power to make for ourselves the laws under which we have to live.'

Published in 1905, the book was a product of its age. Yet in the early twenty-first century, after being out of print for decades, it was resurrected and weaponised. The right-wing think tank Civitas promoted it, and the *Daily Telegraph* raised £25,000 to get it republished and distributed to schools. Future Brexit ideologue Michael Gove, shadow education secretary at the time, appeared to refer to Marshall's book in his 2008 Tory party conference speech: 'Instead of being taught about the Magna Carta, the Glorious Revolution and the heroic role of the Royal Navy in putting down slavery, our children are [now] either taught to put Britain in the dock or they remain in ignorance of our island story. That is morally wrong, culturally self-defeating.' Later, Brexit-enabling prime minister David Cameron revealed himself as another fan. The book had captured his imagination and 'nurtured my interest in the history of our great nation'. The Civitas website looked forward to the day when Marshall would replace 'the truly subversive mush currently taught our schoolchildren in place of proper history'.

By chance, just before this culture war kicked off in earnest, I wrote a book (*Those Feet: A Sensual History of English Football*) about the roots of the English game and became fascinated by its Victorian and Edwardian origins. I realised that the values, obsessions, neuroses and fantasies of that strange period had woven themselves into the fabric and soul of English football, which was invented and promoted in the nineteenth-century public schools to instil imperialist patriotic virtues. These attitudes were never effectively challenged and were with us still, especially in relation to the national team: the sense of innate superiority was deeply ingrained.

Our Island Story was written at the zenith of empire and didn't mention football. It was, though, part of a wider literary culture of patriotic, inspiring stories for children that talked about football a lot. *Boys' Own* and sparsely illustrated Edwardian story papers evolved into later comics such as *Eagle*, *Tiger* and *Victor*. Through idealised fictional heroes such as Dan Dare and Roy of the Rovers, they conveyed obsolete ideas of Englishness to generations of children. Other countries – Brazil, Uruguay and Argentina; Italy, Austria, Hungary, Holland – went on to develop new ways of playing. But the English stuck with what they knew. Football was a rough, tough, noble man's game, a game of war. Strength and speed were celebrated; individualism and creativity were viewed with suspicion. The English had invented the sport and graciously bestowed it upon the world. Naturally, they had to be the best.

Historians have looked in detail at early class tensions in 'the people's game' between working-class professionals and amateur toffs. All good stuff. But I was more intrigued by the way 'manly' imperial values were common to both and remained intact until the Premier League recruited the world's best coaches and players, swamping football's Olde Englishness, thereby changing the elite club game.

Meanwhile, despite the outlier of the 1966 World Cup win (achieved at home with favourable refereeing), England consistently proved they weren't much good at international tournaments. On five occasions after 1966 they failed to reach tournaments at all. When they did qualify, they usually went out in the round of 16 or quarter-final. As Simon Kuper and Stefan Szymanski demonstrated in their 2009 book *Why England Lose*, there was nothing tragic about this: England actually did slightly better than you'd expect given their relatively small talent pool.

Yet the popular (or should I say proto-populist?) media interpreted defeats not as sporting disappointment but as national disgrace. Each tournament elimination was followed by recriminations and a search for scapegoats. As Andrew Anthony remarked in *The Observer*, the phenomenon was so extreme it rewrote Isaac Newton's third law of motion to become: every action has an unequal and hysterical overreaction. This was plainly linked to the wider political and cultural failure to adapt to the post-Second World War loss of empire and geopolitical status. 'Declinism' became established and, while the English became rather good at self-mockery, there was also an edge of real bitterness, a sense of having been cheated of our rightful glory on and off the pitch.

As far as the national team was concerned, the mismatch between the reality of respectable second-rank status and the fantasy that England should always be champions made the business of playing for the team increasingly miserable. The shirt became 'heavy' and star players were routinely singled out for bitter criticism. To cite one minor example, during the 2004 Euros ITV commentator Clive Tyldesley wrote in the *Telegraph* that 'England expects' more of senior players like David Beckham and Michael Owen.

Off the field, by the summer of 2016, some of the people who had promoted an *Our Island Story* vision of Britain were approaching the fulfilment of their dream of leaving the 'tyrannous' European Union. On 23 June, the 'Leave' campaign won the Brexit referendum. The pound crashed, Prime Minister David Cameron resigned, and a sense of bewilderment and chaos engulfed the country.

And four days later, on 27 June, in Nice, not far from the French lands once ruled by the Plantagenet kings, England played Iceland in the European Championship.

Watching old football matches is more like time travel than history. Enter the right search terms, click on the correct Google links and, as if by magic, the world as it was eight years ago appears on a little screen. I'm faintly startled to see Roy Hodgson, looking stressed, as England manager again. England wear that all-white number with red socks and the grey-blue shoulders. I'd half-forgotten this team: 'Broadway' Danny Rose (as I think of him), Gary Cahill, Daniel Sturridge, Joe Hart, sad Dele Alli whose horrific childhood we didn't yet know about. Football time is different: eight years is a generation ago. Wayne Rooney, not yet resembling Henry VIII, is captain.

Before the match, commentators Clive Tyldesley and Glenn Hoddle convey nervousness. Iceland are the overachieving underdogs with amazing fans who do the rhythmic blue Viking thunderclap thing no one's ever seen before. Apparently, they will be hard to break down. Well, yes. To reach the tournament they beat the Czechs, Turkey and the Netherlands (twice). In their group, Iceland beat Austria and drew with Portugal and Hungary. 'The England plan is to play with width and stretch Iceland's doughty defences,' says Clive, but 'on paper, on populations, on any football scale, it's almost a mismatch.' We need an early goal, he reckons. An early goal 'would make such a difference!'

The game starts, and England look OK. They're not exactly Spain 2012, but the passing and moving is competent and they're pinning Iceland back. Youthful Kyle Walker scampers down the right and crosses low. Alli and Raheem Sterling combine on the left. The Iceland goalkeeper fouls Sterling. Sleek young Harry Kane is on the field, but Rooney will take the penalty. Up he runs, and scores neatly into a corner. 'England have their early goal!' exults Clive. 'Lift-off inside four minutes!' 'Perfect start for England!' gurgles Glenn.

But I'm from the future. I know what happens next.

* * *

I cannot stress too much that Britain is part of Europe, and always will be. There will still be intense and intensifying European cooperation and partnership in a huge number of fields: the arts, the sciences, the universities, and on improving the environment. EU citizens living in this country will have their rights fully protected, and the same goes for British citizens living in the EU.

British people will still be able to go and work in the EU; to live; to travel; to study; to buy homes and to settle down. As the German equivalent of the CBI – the BDI – has very sensibly reminded us, there will continue to be free trade, and access to the single market. Britain is and always will be a great European power, offering top-table opinions and giving leadership on everything from foreign policy to defence to counter-terrorism and intelligence-sharing - all the things we need to do together to make our world safer.

The only change - and it will not come in any great rush - is that the UK will extricate itself from the EU's extraordinary and opaque system of legislation: the vast and growing corpus of law enacted by a European Court of Justice from which there can be no appeal. This will bring not threats, but golden opportunities for this country - to pass laws and set taxes according to the needs of the UK.

Boris Johnson, *Daily Telegraph*, 27 June 2016

* * *

Britain has lost its final gold-plated AAA rating, following Standard & Poor's decision to downgrade the country by two notches, to AA.

S&P warned that the Brexit vote will lead to 'less predictable, stable, and effective policy framework in the UK' and hurt growth.

Fitch, another major credit rating, has also downgraded Britain to AA tonight, from AA+.

The moves came after another day of losses on the stock markets. The FTSE 100 index lost another 156 points, while medium-sized companies on the FTSE 250 fell by 6%.

Banking shares suffered most, amid fears of a UK recession, with Royal Bank of Scotland plunging by 25% at one point.

The pound hit a new 31-year low against the US dollar, despite chancellor George Osborne trying to calm the market panic over the EU referendum vote.

***The Guardian*, 27 June 2016**

* * *

Brexit crisis: Move to depose Labour leader

In the early hours of yesterday, Mr Corbyn sacked Shadow Foreign Secretary Hilary Benn for 'disloyalty' after it was revealed he rang Shadow Cabinet colleagues in the aftermath of Thursday's Brexit vote to gauge support for a coup attempt.

Eleven members of the Shadow Cabinet then quit in protest at Mr Corbyn's failure to inspire enough Labour voters to back Remain.

In a scathing resignation letter, departing Shadow Leader of the Commons Chris Bryant said: 'Your ambivalent attitude in the campaign was a betrayal of the Labour Party ... and it has let down a whole generation of young people.'

Mr Bryant concluded: 'If you refuse to step aside, I fear you will go down in history as the man who broke the Labour Party.'

The astonishing mass walkout, just the latest rumble of Britain's post-Brexit earthquake, was organised via a secret group on the WhatsApp messaging service and played out at staged intervals throughout the day.

It is understood a second wave of up to 20 junior Shadow ministers will resign today unless Mr Corbyn steps down.

***Daily Mirror*, 27 June 2016**

2
Our Iceland Story: The Next 86 Minutes

THIRTY-FOUR SECONDS after the restart, Iceland equalise from a long throw. Olde England knew how to defend long throws but, as Glenn Hoddle says on commentary, the current generation aren't used to 1980s-style football and don't know how to counter it. Most of the England team play in club sides packed with technical and tactical sophisticates from around the world. Their club coaches are thoroughly modern Millies, too. Under a succession of England managers – Terry Venables, Hoddle himself, Roy Hodgson to a degree – the national team has learned to play a more modern European style.

Then Iceland score again. A smooth attack ends with the ball at the feet of Kolbeinn Sigthorsson on the edge of the England penalty area, and he tries his luck with a shot. As Joe Hart dives to his left to make the relatively simple save, my mind skips back to an earlier England keeper who dived to make a relatively simple save. Poor Peter Bonetti – usually excellent and only playing because Gordon Banks had food poisoning – was thrown with minimal preparation into the legendary/notorious 1970 World Cup quarter-final against West Germany in Mexico. With 21 minutes to go and England comfortably winning 2-0, Franz Beckenbauer tried his luck from a similar distance: a modest effort that Bonetti fumbled. England went on to lose 2-3 and failed to qualify for another major tournament for ten years. Long after Bonetti had retired, total strangers felt entitled to come up and tell him he'd 'lost the World Cup'. And now it was big Joe Hart's turn. He got his hands to the shot but it squirmed over the line. He was 'shit'. He 'let us down'. He was arrogant and overpaid.

Hart's mistake should not have been fatal. Of the two teams, England had much better and more experienced players. With a bit of calm and intelligently applied skill, they would surely have pulled back an equaliser and gone on to win the tie. But England began to rush and snatch and worry. Teamwork fell apart. By the second half, the entire team was in the grip of a nervous breakdown and reverting to a parodic version of kick and rush. Basic technique deserted them. Long balls were hoisted pointlessly and inaccurately to the box; simple passes went miles astray or were miscontrolled. England didn't manage a single shot on target. The nadir, near the end, was a Kane free kick that ballooned hopelessly into the crowd.

The reaction was predictably measured and balanced. It was 'a disgrace', 'a fucking disgrace', 'humiliation', 'our greatest humiliation', 'the worst defeat in our history' (Lineker), 'the worst performance I've ever seen from an England team' (Alan Shearer), and in its player ratings *The Times* gave every England player a zero.

I saw the way England played as a kind of mad performance-art piece in which the political and economic chaos caused by the Brexit referendum manifested in flesh and grass. Were the players supposed to be looking to the future and playing like modern Europeans? Or were they regressing?

Others saw it as 'Brexit football'. Exultant Icelandic TV commentator Gudmundur Benediktsson certainly noticed a connection: 'Live the way you want, England! Iceland is going to play France. France–Iceland! You can go home. You can go out of Europe. You can go wherever the hell you want.'

The players themselves viewed it in more personal terms: they had frozen with fear of the inevitable hammering they'd get from fans and media if they lost. The England shirt had become as heavy as medieval chain mail.

Paul Hayward, in his book *England Football: The Biography*, talks of the 'morbid fear of the consequences of failure' that by 2016 was transmitting itself 'virus-like' from one generation of England players to the next. He quotes Steven Gerrard's explanation of what happens to England players when things begin to go wrong:

> Your mind drifts to what the coverage is going to be like back home and the level of criticism you are going to get. You cannot stop yourself. What if we don't get back into this? What will it be like if we go out here?

> Panic sets in. The frustration takes over. You freeze and stop doing those things you know you should be doing. You start forcing the game, making the wrong choices with your passes, shooting from the wrong areas and letting the anxiety prevent you from doing the simple things. Everything you said and prepared for before the game gets forgotten.

Either way, Our Iceland Story had shown that living with one foot in a mythologised past couldn't work. The neuroses attending the *Our Island Story*-style fantasies around the England team were no longer sustainable. Something would have to change.

* * *

Survey finds worsening of U.S. race relations: Few Americans harbor hope for improvements from Black Lives Matter

Black and white Americans experience life in profoundly and persistently different ways, according to a new Pew Research Center survey examining racial attitudes in the United States.

The telephone survey, conducted over a three-month period starting in February, is the latest in a series of polls by various organizations trying to make sense of the sharp deterioration in the country's optimistic racial attitudes since the election of the nation's first black president in 2008. While most African-Americans think individual racism is a bigger factor than institutional racism, they also say they have experienced unfair treatment by a number of institutions.

***New York Times*, 28 June 2016**

* * *

Muslim group 'extremely concerned' about racist attacks following Brexit

Members of the Ahmadiyya Muslim community are opening the doors of the Noor Mosque in Langley Green to the public in a bid to counter 'Brexit hate messages.'

The move follows an incident earlier this month when graffiti was daubed on the doors of the mosque in Langley Drive.

In a statement this week, regional president Ahsan Ahmedi said: 'In light of last Thursday's

Europe Referendum and the consequence of a Brexit win, the Ahmadiyya Muslim community in Crawley is extremely concerned at some adverse racist reaction against some ethnic communities in the UK.

'Having recently suffered some hate graffiti at the Noor Mosque only recently, members of the Ahmadiyya Muslim community are extremely concerned that such sentiments can surface again.'

***Crawley Observer*, 30 June 2016**

* * *

1.2 million child deaths that India could have prevented

New Delhi – Around 1.2 million children died of preventable causes in India in 2015 before celebrating their fifth birthday, a Unicef report has said in a grim reminder of the abysmal state of child healthcare in the world's fastest growing major economy.

Most of the deaths were caused by diseases easily preventable and treatable, says the report released Tuesday that counts India among the five countries accounting for half the 5.9 million under-five deaths reported across the world last year.

The other four countries are Democratic Republic of Congo, Ethiopia, Nigeria and Pakistan, whose economies are smaller when compared with India's. ...

Sanitation can go a long way in preventing these deaths, especially those caused by diarrhoea. The report says while 94% of the Indian population has access to clean drinking water, toilet facilities are available to only 40% of the people.

Proper nutrition, immunisation and safe water, too, can substantially bring down the deaths. The UN children's agency has stressed on educating girls. If all mothers complete secondary education, South Asia will see 1.3 million fewer child deaths every year, it says.

***Hindustan Times*, 28 June 2016**

3
Boring Guys

3 October 2016

I DON'T remember if it was a Christmas party, but it was definitely late 2015 when my friend invited me to a social event at the Kentish Town branch of the Labour Party. I wasn't keen but she said there'd be some cool people and a chance to meet their new MP, who was interesting. I'd been vaguely aware of him for years but hadn't given him much thought or seen him up close. It was a febrile moment in the Labour Party, and the mood in the branch was close to mutinous. Activist members had known Jeremy Corbyn, MP for a nearby constituency, for years, never liked him much, and were horrified he'd recently become party leader largely thanks to support from a massive influx of new members.

The social in Kentish Town was a low-key affair: an amiable raffle, some food and, as promised, interesting people to chat to. And then came the bit that stands out in my memory. The new MP stood up to speak. Former Director of Public Prosecutions Sir Keir Starmer, who'd only formally entered politics a few months earlier and been elected for the constituency of which Kentish Town was a part, didn't say much about the issue of the day. He didn't mention Corbyn by name, and he spoke without a hint of oratorical flourish or even jokes. But his message was clear, calm, reasonable and so emphatically persuasive it closed off even the possibility of disagreement. I wish I could remember his exact words because they were skilful, but the gist was this: the leadership decision was definitive and had to be fully respected. Whatever differences of opinion or reservations people may have must be put aside. In the coming months and years, what was needed in the party was a spirit of mutual respect and comradeship and working together. In time, Starmer would be mocked for being boring, for lacking charisma, for being a centrist 'Blairite'. His enemies on the left would call him 'Keith', claim he was nothing but a 'red Tory', and 'traitor'. But I remember thinking: there's something about this guy. He's really rather good.

Back in the parallel world of football, Roy Hodgson had resigned as England manager immediately after the Iceland defeat and been replaced by the ebullient, Brexit-voting Sam Allardyce, the former Blackpool, Notts County, Bolton, Newcastle, Blackburn, West Ham and Sunderland boss. 'Big Sam' (not to be confused with 'Big Mal' or 'Big Ron', managerial flamboyants of the past) was a straight-talking populist. Four years earlier, he'd claimed to be joking when he said he would never be allowed to run a top English club because his name did not sound Italian ('I won't ever be going to a top-four club because I'm not called Allardici'). Friends and colleagues insisted he was a more sophisticated football thinker than he appeared. But he was more than happy to send up his reputation as a shouty old-school gaffer. A 2005 TV advert, for example, showed him haranguing his underperforming team, furiously telling them to 'grow up'. When the camera pulls back we see he's shouting at a bunch of bewildered ten-year-olds. At his first England press conference he was brash and confident: 'I think I fit the chair' ... 'Bring it on, eh lads, I'm hardened over many, many years.' But he also talked in a modern manner about psychology, lifting the psychological pressure on players, and making playing for England enjoyable: 'We are all together, trying to create a good team spirit and have some fun. The game of football is to be enjoyed and I have enjoyed my life in the game for many years now.'

Two months after getting the job he was on camera again, secretly filmed by *Daily Telegraph* reporters posing as businessmen. Sam drank wine from a pint glass, mocked his predecessor, offered to 'get around' rules on player transfers, and asked for £400,000 to be a 'keynote speaker' to promote a fake company to Far East investors. Resignation 'by mutual agreement' followed swiftly and Gareth Southgate, manager of the Under-21s, was appointed interim manager.

Gareth's first public act in the role was a press conference. I remembered him as a player, of course – good defender, missed that penalty against Germany in '96 – but I'd never thought about him much as a manager of Middlesbrough or with the

England Under-21s. As he spoke, I noticed a few middle-management fillers ('just really to say', 'at this moment in time', 'lots of positives') but he was impressive. In years to come he would be called boring, cautious and centrist. He didn't crack jokes or big himself up, and he handled reporters' questions with care and intelligence. Modest but steely, he refused to be drawn into criticising Sam Allardyce or saying he wanted the job permanently. He praised his young players and then-captain Wayne Rooney. He declared himself 'a proud and patriotic Englishman' and said it was an 'honour' to be England manager, even temporarily. His only objective for now was to prepare his team in the best way possible to win their remaining qualifying matches for the 2018 World Cup. And then, near the end, came a flash of something else, something heartfelt and resonant. He even said it twice: 'I'm involved in a sport that I love and an industry that at times I don't like.' And a few moments later: 'I think there's lots about the industry of football that I don't like, but it's a sport I love.'

I remember thinking: there's something about this guy. He's really rather good.

* * *

Horoscope: Virgo

Stay with what is known and familiar to you, at least until the end of the month. Refuse to allow one particular person's restlessness to lure you from something that's slowly coming to fruition.

Harper's Bazaar New York, October 2016
[Gareth Southgate is a Virgo]

* * *

[Sam] Allardyce was due to announce his squad for the next round of qualifiers on Sunday but now Southgate will be in charge for four matches against Malta at Wembley (8 October), Slovenia away (11 October), Scotland at home (11 November) and Spain in a friendly (15 November) as the FA searches for a successor.

Southgate ruled himself out of the running for the England manager job prior to Allardyce's appointment but the current bookmakers' favourite may become a contender, depending on results in his caretaker spell.

Bournemouth's Eddie Howe, Crystal Palace manager Alan Pardew and former Hull City boss Steve Bruce are also among the possible candidates.

BBC News, 27 September 2017

* * *

One hundred days after the British referendum, the Prime Minister announced her roadmap for Brexit on Sunday. London will initiate the legal procedure to leave the Union in March 2017. The United Kingdom will undertake a vast legislative project to achieve a final divorce in spring 2019. Theresa May insisted on the 'sovereignty' and 'independence' of a country called to play 'a new role in the world'.

***Le Monde*, 3 October 2016**

* * *

Putin suspends nuclear pact, raising stakes in row with Washington

Russian President Vladimir Putin on Monday suspended a treaty with Washington on cleaning up weapons-grade plutonium, signalling he is willing to use nuclear disarmament as a new bargaining chip in disputes with the United States over Ukraine and Syria.

Starting in the last years of the Cold War, Russia and the United States signed a series of accords to reduce the size of their nuclear arsenals, agreements that have so far survived intact despite a souring of U.S.-Russian relations under Putin.

But on Monday, Putin issued a decree suspending an agreement, concluded in 2000, which bound the two sides to dispose of surplus plutonium originally intended for use in nuclear weapons.

The Kremlin said it was taking that action in response to unfriendly acts by Washington. It made the announcement shortly before Washington said it was suspending talks with Russia on trying to end the violence in Syria.

The plutonium accord is not the cornerstone of post-Cold War U.S.-Russia disarmament, and the practical implications from the suspension will be limited. But the suspension, and the linkage to disagreements on other issues, carries powerful symbolism.

Reuters, 3 October 2016

4
Endings and Beginnings

11 October 2016

'SOMETIMES BEFORE we can usher in the new, the old must be put to rest.' Doesn't sound too terrible, does it? But it's the scene in *Game of Thrones* where sinister, soft-spoken Master of Whisperers, backed by a gaggle of scary children, is speaking gently to the white-bearded Grand Maester. The Whisperer just said, 'I bear you no ill will', which is a very bad sign.

James Graham's play *Dear England* imagines an equivalent scene between Gareth Southgate and Wayne Rooney. Wayne mentions the talented young players emerging in the UK: 'It's great, you know, all these new kids coming up. Look at a lot of 'em, and I'm like, wow. Great.' Gareth, awkward rather than sinister, says: 'Good. Yeah. I suppose... I've got some ideas of what I think we might need to do, here, to seize this moment with... exactly, some newer, younger...'

In *Game of Thrones*, the talented kids step from the shadows and very horribly stab the Grand Maester to death. In our game of throw-ins, Gareth dropped the closest thing English football had to a grand master.[1] No blood spurted, but a dramatic sudden ending is a dramatic sudden ending all the same.

Rooney at the time wasn't the force he'd been at his peak, and he was in poor form for Manchester United. But the greatest English player of the age was still captain of England, had a record number of goals for his country and more caps than any other outfield player. He was still only 30, expected to remain a key figure with the national team for another couple of years and to retire after the 2018 World Cup. Moreover, he'd just captained the side in Gareth's first match in charge, a qualifier against Malta that England won 2-0. Three days later, on the morning of the game away to Slovenia, Gareth put the knife in. The former captain would be on the subs'

---

1 Not my pun: @GameofThrowIns was someone's Twitter handle.

bench, Jordan Henderson would take the armband, Dele Alli the number 10 role. England played badly and were lucky to escape with a scoreless draw.

Gareth said the decision to drop Wayne was 'tactical' and a year later, with the player now back at Everton, his boyhood club, Gareth asked him to come back to fill a gap left by an injury to Adam Lallana. Wayne declined and announced his international retirement.[2]

Media reaction back in 2016 was largely positive. Chris Sutton praised Gareth for having the 'gumption' to drop Rooney after Roy Hodgson and Sam Allardyce had kept him in the team. Daniel Taylor said Gareth had 'done the sensible thing': 'English football loved the assassin-faced baby but the days have passed since he made us quicken our step *en route* to wherever he was playing. What we are left with now is a fading old pro, approaching his 31st birthday.'

But the players took a slightly different message from the episode. As Danny Rose later observed: 'I

---

2 As it happened, he did play once more: a 32-minute cameo in 2018, in a friendly against the USA in what was effectively a charity match for his Wayne Rooney Foundation.

definitely didn't expect the manager to drop him against Slovenia, and as soon as we all saw that we knew that that gaffer was not somebody to be messed around with. It was a huge shock for all of us … You know he has this nice side to him but at the same time he has a side that you don't want to cross. It literally is: buy into what he and his coaching staff believe or he won't choose you. You either want to be here or you don't. If you are here, you have to get on board with everything.'

* * *

Poll: After Trump tape revelation, Clinton's lead up to double digits

As Donald Trump's campaign reels over tapes of the presidential candidate's sexually aggressive comments about women in 2005, the Republican nominee now trails Hillary Clinton by double digits among likely voters, according to a new NBC News/Wall Street Journal poll. The poll, conducted on Saturday and Sunday but before the second presidential debate, shows Clinton with 46 percent support among likely voters in a four-way matchup, compared to 35 percent for Trump.

Libertarian Gary Johnson's support stands at nine percent, and Green Party candidate Jill Stein garners two percent. In a head-to-head matchup, Clinton's lead over Trump grows to 14 percent (52 percent to Trump's 38 percent.) And among all registered voters, Clinton's lead is 13 points, her largest advantage over Trump since the poll began testing the pair last September.

As Republicans grapple with how to hold on to control of the House and Senate despite the Trump campaign's woes, Democrats overall now have a seven-point advantage on the question of which party voters want to see in control of Congress.

Forty-nine percent of voters say they'd like to see Democrats in power on Capitol Hill, compared to 42 percent who chose the GOP.

NBC News, 11 October 2016

* * *

Ruth Bader Ginsburg says national anthem protests are 'really dumb'

Santa Clara, Calif. – Supreme Court Justice Ruth Bader Ginsburg is not a believer in protesting by sitting or kneeling during the national anthem.

Speaking to Yahoo! on Monday morning, Ginsburg had some harsh words for San Francisco 49ers quarterback Colin Kaepernick and other players who have decided to kneel during the national anthem in protest of racial inequality.

'I think it's really dumb of them,' Ginsburg said. 'Would I arrest them for doing it? No. I think it's dumb and disrespectful. I would have the same answer if you asked me about flag burning. I think it's a terrible thing to do, but I wouldn't lock a person up for doing it.

'I would point out how ridiculous it seems to me to do such an act. But it's dangerous to arrest people for conduct that doesn't jeopardize the health or well-being of other people. It's a symbol they're engaged in.'

Kaepernick began his protest in August by sitting during the national anthem before the first three preseason games. After a meeting with Army Green Beret Nate Boyer, Kaepernick decided to kneel in an effort to make the protest more respectful.

Safety Eric Reid joined Kaepernick then and linebacker Eli Harold has also begun kneeling in the past few weeks. Other NFL players have also joined in kneeling or by raising their right fists during the playing of 'The Star-Spangled Banner.'

ESPN, 10 October 2016

* * *

What can you do with Vladimir Putin?

Left-leaning *Libération* puts the Russian President Vladimir Putin on its front page. Vlad is due here in Paris later this month and is expecting to talk to François Hollande about the Syrian conflict and the Ukrainian crisis. But it's not clear that the French president is going to be available.

Yesterday French leaders accused Russian forces of bombing the Syrian city of Aleppo, saying that such action clearly constituted a war crime, adding that those who commit war crimes have to accept responsibility, even before the International Criminal Court.

Does that mean Putin risks being arrested and transferred to the Hague if he shows up in Paris on 19 October?

Right-wing paper *Le Figaro* is running a readers' poll on the question of whether Hollande should or should not meet Putin in Paris. With 48,000 votes, 78 percent were in favour of the planned meeting going ahead.

Le Figaro's analysis of the situation points to Russia's weekend veto of a French call at the UN Security Council for an end to the bombing of Aleppo, leaving no room for ambiguity about the Kremlin's determination to continue to support Bashar al-Assad's regime in Syria, whatever the international consequences.

Radio France International, 11 October 2016

5
Military Men

2 June 2017

ROB DRAPER and Jonathan Northcroft's *Dear England* kicks off with an account of one of his most revealing team-building exercises. On the morning of Friday, 2 June 2017, the players assembled in a dressing room at St George's Park. 'They were midway through a presentation when the door burst open and through it stepped a Royal Marine. Leave everything, even phones, he said, and don't tell anyone where you are going. The players were allowed one text – to loved ones, to say they would not be contactable for the next 48 hours.'

What followed was immersion – literally – in a world of muddy, character-building military-grade discomfort on a Marines' training course that reads like an English version of the first half of *Full Metal Jacket* (albeit with less bullying, murder or ingestion of jelly doughnuts).

Players and staff alike were given camouflage outfits, backpacks, sleeping mats and boots and trucked to a remote location in Devon. There they smeared mud on their faces, received standard Marine rations, set up camp among the trees and prepared for two gruelling days of yomping, stream-wading, lugging heavy items over a tower, and assaults on a fake house using paintball guns. Some of the exercises seem rooted in collective memories of the nightmarish conditions of the First World War. The players split into pairs for the 'drop and drag', with one man playing unconscious and the other hauling his dead weight along a mud path. Entering the 'sheep dip' meant trusting a comrade to pull you to safety from underneath thick, foul, muddy water. A third involved wading waist-deep along a river while holding a rope but having to duck completely underwater every time a whistle blew. The whistle, of course, would have reminded the players of a referee's whistle. But it also carried a dark ancestral military echo. During the near-suicidal mass attacks of the First World War, British officers blew whistles to signal that it was time to leave the trenches and walk towards barbed wire and German machine guns.

In line with the ethos that no commander should ask his men to do something he wouldn't do himself, Gareth insisted on going first on every exercise. He hoped the experience would help cultivate an ethos of mutual dependency and solidarity, a sense of 'the importance of the person next to you'. And it seems to have worked. Confounding the popular image of modern football stars as pampered and self-absorbed, the England men threw themselves wholeheartedly into their tasks and seem to have loved the weekend. Raheem Sterling recalled: 'I felt like it was another stepping stone that brought everyone closer together.'

It also linked Gareth to his beloved late grandfather on his mother's side. From Arthur Toll, a Royal Marine and Second World War veteran, Gareth had learned fierce patriotism, a sense of duty and the notion of serving his nation. It was in his grandfather's honour that Gareth wore his famous waistcoat during the 2018 World Cup.

Training with the Royal Marines connected Gareth and the players to one of the wellsprings of English football. Perhaps 'reconnected' might be a better word, for the martial element is central not only to the Toll/Southgate family but to the history of the English game, which developed from the testosterone-drenched 'folk football' that once flourished around Britain. These medieval games were wild, carnivalesque, Catholic semi-riots typically involving hundreds of men on each side brawling through countryside, villages and towns. Reflecting an old English love of fighting, the only rule of the game at Atherstone, for example, is that you're not allowed to kill an opponent.

The Industrial Revolution largely ended folk football, though it survived in a handful of remote places such as Ashbourne in Derbyshire. Through the nineteenth century, however, the sport evolved, undergoing a radical Protestant transformation in a handful of elite public schools. Thanks to several powerful and influential headmasters, slimmed-down versions of the game were reinvented as an educational tool. Ferocious by today's standards, football began to be recognisably modern. The number of players on each team was radically reduced and elaborate rules were adopted. Because these varied between schools, by the middle of the nineteenth century players who had moved on to university needed universal rules so they could play together. The process led, in 1863, to the formation of the Football Association, which – thanks to player-administrators such as C.W. Alcock – in turn spawned the FA Cup and international matches, beginning with England v Scotland. All modern football derives from these developments.

Meanwhile, back in the schools, in the jingoistic, imperialist atmosphere of the late nineteenth century, the sporting ethos took an ideological turn. The new sports were designed to instil the idea of the natural superiority of Englishmen, and to teach imperialist warrior values to boys who would one day lead and staff the British army and administer the Empire. The point of football was not mere fun but to teach morality, teamwork, discipline, pluck and courage. From the public schools and Oxbridge, these values were later evangelised to the working class through football. Many of today's Premier League teams, including Manchester City, started out as church sides promoting 'muscular Christianity'.

The apotheosis of this culture came almost 100 years to the day before England's Euro 2016 game against Iceland. The most famous story concerns a 21-year-old officer in the East Surrey regiment called Wilfred 'Billie' Nevill. Son of a coal merchant, he had played hockey, football and cricket at his school, Dover College, before going on to Jesus College, Cambridge to read classics. There the college magazine, writing of his prowess on the football field, drew attention to a weakness later common to generations of English centre-halves: 'His tackling is brilliant but he does not help his forwards too cleverly.'

When the Great War came, he enrolled and quickly rose to the rank of captain. A keen photographer, he took pictures with his unit on the Western Front. Just two years earlier he had posed, carefree and happy, wearing a sports blazer at Cambridge. In Flanders he looks to have aged at least a decade. He's grown a fine military moustache, and poses with comrades and alone. In several pictures he's wearing a gas mask; in others he's smoking a cigarette, having his hair cut, or looking sombre in a trench or behind sandbags. On a trip home in May 1916, knowing he would soon be involved in the 'big push' that history calls the Battle of the Somme, he visited a sporting goods store and purchased two leather footballs. When the whistles blew, he reasoned, it would be good for the morale of his men to be able to kick the balls towards the German lines at Montauban. The balls were later retrieved from the battlefield. One was inscribed: 'The Great European Cup, The Final, East Surreys v Bavarians, Kick Off at Zero'. The other, in large letters, read: 'NO REFEREE'. In a letter written later to Wilfred's sister, his friend and fellow officer C.W. Alcock[3] explained what happened:

> I feel you would like to know all you possibly can about Wilfred and the truly plucky way he was killed ... Five minutes before 'zero' time (7.30 am) your brother strolled up in his usual calm way, and we shared a last joke before going over. The company went over the

---

3 Not the C.W. Alcock who invented the FA Cup and international football.

> top very well, with Soames and your brother kicking off with the Company footballs. We had to face a very heavy rifle and machine gun fire, and nearing the front German trench, the lines slackened 'pace' slightly. Seeing this, Wilfred dashed in front with a bomb in his hand, and was immediately shot through the heart, almost side by side with Soames and Sergeant Major Wells. As you probably know, we found him on the following Monday, and he was buried in the Soldiers' Cemetery at Carnoy. Evans was killed also.

Football and death were no less entwined in the 'football battalion', the 17th Middlesex, which was formed in 1914 and made up almost entirely of footballers. As Andrew Riddoch and John Kemp reveal in distressing detail in their book *When the Whistle Blows*, few of these sporting soldiers survived. Recruited to fight the 'game of games against one of the finest teams in the world', they were mown down in their hundreds: 500 died in three weeks on the Somme, 300 at Redan Ridge, and 462 at Oppy.

Even now, English football journalism and TV and radio commentary loves its martial language. A season or qualification tournament is a 'campaign'; teams 'blitz' their opponents; a flying forward 'leads the charge'; a tough team-mate is 'exactly the sort of player you'd want with you in the trenches'. It's all a dim echo of the kind of stuff that swirled around the battalion.

One of the officers was Walter Tull, Britain's first Black footballer. Joe Mercer, Nottingham Forest's centre-half, was sergeant major to battalion commander Major Frank Buckley, who later managed Wolves. Mercer was wounded (some say gassed, but his son said it was his shoulder) and held in a prisoner-of-war camp for 18 months.

After the war he played part-time for Tranmere Rovers alongside the young Dixie Dean. His health never fully recovered from the war, but he lived long enough to imbue his son, also called Joe, with a love of football and country. Joe Mercer the younger played for Everton in the 1930s, Arsenal in the late 1940s and 1950s and, during the Second World War, became a sergeant major in the army. In the late 1960s he managed the great Manchester City of

Book and Bell, and in 1974, between the reigns of Alf Ramsey and Don Revie, became one of Gareth Southgate's best-loved predecessors as caretaker manager of England.

Mercer was hardly unusual. For decades, a military background was practically de rigueur for England managers. Walter Winterbottom was a wing commander in the RAF during the Second World War; Alf Ramsey served in the Duke of Cornwall's Light Infantry; Don Revie did two years' Army National Service; Ron Greenwood was in the RAF, and Bobby Robson would have served were it not for his partial deafness. In other words, there was nothing whimsical or tokenistic about Gareth Southgate's Royal Marines training weekend. He was updating and reinvigorating one of the most potent and evocative strands of English football history.

* * *

Seven people have been killed and at least 48 injured in a terror incident in London in which three male attackers were shot dead by police.

A white van hit pedestrians on London Bridge at about 22:00 BST on Saturday, then three men got out and stabbed people in nearby Borough Market. Police said the three men were wearing fake bomb vests. ...

Political parties have suspended national general election campaigning and the prime minister is chairing a meeting of the government's Cobra emergency committee. Theresa May described Saturday night's events as 'dreadful', while Labour leader Jeremy Corbyn called them 'brutal and shocking'.

Borough Market is an area known for its bars and restaurants which were busy on a warm summer evening. London Mayor Sadiq Khan said it was 'a deliberate and cowardly attack on innocent Londoners', but the capital remained the 'safest global city' and Londoners would not be cowed by terrorism.

It is the third terror attack in the UK in three months following the car and knife attack in Westminster in March, which left five people dead, and the Manchester bombing less than two weeks ago, in which 22 people were killed.

BBC News, 4 June 2017

* * *

'I was watching the game in a bar in Via Po that had set up screens on the street. I was leaving the bathroom when the screaming crowd (they said someone was shooting wildly, which wasn't true) pushed me back inside, and we locked ourselves in ... The bar staff closed all the shutters and in the street you could see people running, screaming and banging on the shutters to get them to open. So we locked ourselves in the bathroom again with people screaming and crying. After about 10 minutes, the owner sent us to the cellar and we were there for about half an hour, then they started saying that it was nothing. Some people tried to call 112 but for more than five minutes no one answered. Total panic. Luckily, we were quite far away, but locked down there we didn't know anything and all we could hear was a lot of sirens, which made us fear the worst. Many were crying, there would have been about 40 of us in the cellars.'

***Corriere della Sera,* 4 June 2017**

[Eyewitness Federico Baldassarri describing deadly panic in Turin during the Champions League final between Juventus and Real Madrid, the same night as the London Bridge murders. More than 1,500 people were injured (three later died) after a group of men released pepper spray in a crowd watching the match in Piazza San Carlo.]

* * *

TULL – March 25th, killed in action in France. Second-Lieut. Walter D. Tull. Middlesex. Youngest son of the late Mr. Daniel Tull of Folkestone, aged 29 years. Deeply mourned by his brothers and sisters.

***Folkestone, Hythe, Sandgate & Cheriton Herald*, 13 April 1918**

6
Bus Stops

3 July 2018

SOME CALLED it 'the Love Train', but it reminded me more of the films of Esther Williams, Hollywood's graceful pioneer of synchronised swimming. When England won a corner, four or five attackers would form a neat, expectant queue near the edge of the penalty area. As the ball floated in, the players would spin into prearranged patterns to baffle and overwhelm the defence. With a decoy run here, and a block or leap there, it was hard to stop. The choreography was so beautiful that I still think of Harry Maguire as a million-dollar mermaid. Sadly, the co-inventor of this lovely manoeuvre had a more prosaic name for it. Allan Russell called it 'the bus stop', and it was the source of an improbable number of goals for England at the World Cup in Russia.

As the *Telegraph*'s Jason Burt reported at the time, Gareth – more than any previous England manager – gleaned tactical, technical and psychological insights from other sports. He was an 'ideas magpie' and 'a sponge when it comes to tactical gains and simply thinking differently'. He was fascinated by NFL football, spoke often to England rugby coach Eddie Jones, and studied cricket, athletics, boxing, swimming and even speed skating. The idea for what became the bus stop seems to have come from a visit to the USA in February 2018 to watch the Super Bowl and take in a Minnesota Timberwolves NBA game. Intrigued by the basketball players' 'screening' and space-making, Gareth wondered if such tactics could be applied in football and asked Allan Russell, who he'd recruited as a strikers' coach, to see if he could make it work.

Four years later, in an article for The Coaches' Voice website, Russell explained some of his training methods: 'We started working on target areas and timing of runs. I had my delivery guys who put in ball after ball. We worked incredibly hard on their delivery. When we started off, we were hitting the target areas around 30 per cent of the time. By the end of the World Cup, we'd got that up to 88 per cent. We aligned that accuracy with the desired angle and height of the delivery and well-timed movements in the box. On top of that, we did a lot of research into our opponents.' Kieran Trippier or, sometimes, Ashley Young took the corners (absurdly, under Roy Hodgson and Sam Allardyce it had been Harry Kane's job). Jordan Henderson organised the bus queue, Raheem Sterling became a screening expert, and the preferred outcome of the exercise was for the ball to reach the bonces of John Stones, Maguire or Kane.

Before Russia, England had failed to score from any of their previous 72 major tournament corners. Now, as the first group game against Tunisia demonstrated, corners became England's deadliest weapon. In the first half, the Tunisian goalkeeper stopped Stones' direct header from one corner, but Kane swept in the rebound. The late winner was more impressive still. Deep in injury time, the score was 1-1 and England, as at many earlier World Cups, seemed about to demoralise themselves by dropping points against low-ranked opponents. Then they won a corner and Russell strode from the dugout and shouted: 'BUS STOP!' Obediently, the players formed their neat queue beyond the penalty spot and Trippier delivered a rehearsed cross. As his team-mates leapt, spun and blocked, Maguire rose at the near post to guide the ball to the far post where Kane, somehow imparting a corkscrew motion to the ball, headed in with the flourish of a craftsman.

In the exhilarating and unexpected run to the semi-final that followed, England scored a total of 12 goals, nine of them from set pieces. Four came from corners, with three more from penalties (two for fouls at corners), and two free kicks. It was a triumph of preparation: Gareth Southgate's hard work, meticulous research, attention to detail, collaborative spirit and his eagerness to embrace new ideas.

'England are the kings of the set piece so far at this World Cup, and it is something to be proud of,' wrote Alan Shearer after two games, hinting in a get-your-retaliation-in-first sort of way that some people might not be proud. Critics were more explicit: reliance on set pieces masked a weakness. Of course, being good at set plays is better than being bad at set plays, but truly great tournament-winning teams tend to be able to conjure goals from a variety of methods and from open play. The obsession with set pieces suggested the mindset of canny mid-table scrappers, of underdogs making the most of limited resources, of Tony Pulis and Rory Delap at Stoke.

The nation didn't mind. Back home during that heady summer the public grew increasingly ecstatic as Gareth's boys Esther Williamsed their way deep into the tournament. Getting outplayed for long periods of the round-of-16 game by Colombia was a sign that all might not be perfect, but England hung on in that match and even – thrilling novelty! – won the penalty shoot-out. (Allan Russell had been helping them on that too.)

After bludgeoning a limited Sweden side in the quarter-final, England finally ran into a team of greater creative range. Wondrously, England took the lead after just five minutes (with a set piece, natch: a Trippier free kick). But after that they only managed one other shot on target over the next 115 minutes. By the second half, Croatia had worked out how to neutralise the bus stop and were overrunning England in midfield. Luka Modrić and Ivan Rakitić created a steady stream of complex movement through the centre and down each wing. Nothing in England's preparation had equipped them to deal with wave after wave of that sort of thing. England looked out of their depth. They began to drown. Croatia won 2-1.

* * *

Did Jeremy Corbyn miss his stop at PMQs by talking buses, not Brexit?

Theresa May has a cabinet and party bitterly divided by Brexit, while one of her top ministers has been forced to apologise for misleading MPs over the government's flagship benefits shake-up.

So Jeremy Corbyn asked the prime minister about buses.

The Labour leader's choice of questions at Prime Minister's Questions prompted claims from critics that, unlike England's footballers in Russia,

Mr Corbyn had missed yet another open goal; or, perhaps, missed his stop.

Rather than put Mrs May under pressure over her warring party's splits on the nature of the UK's departure from the EU, or raise public criticism from Whitehall's spending watchdog of Work and Pensions Secretary Esther McVey, the Labour leader devoted all six of his allotted questions to what he termed a bus services 'crisis'.

Mr Corbyn was heckled with shouts of 'taxi' from the Tory benches as he continued to plough on without mentioning Brexit, while commentators suggested Mrs May will have been sighing a huge sigh of relief.

Sky News online, 4 July 2018

* * *

Catch the Bus Week 2018 underway

Buses Minister Nusrat Ghani MP launched the 6th annual celebration of bus travel with a photocall at Westminster. …

Catch the Bus Week - spearheaded by Greener Journeys - aims to raise awareness of the vast economic, environmental and social benefits of taking the bus. The initiative, now in its 6th year, urges passengers, bus operators and local authorities to work together to encourage the switch from car to bus.

Nusrat Ghani, the Buses Minister, said: 'Whether commuting to work or seeing friends and family, buses play an important role in keeping communities connected with 4.4 billion passenger journeys a year. Choosing the bus is a better decision for the environment and also eases congestion on the road as well as speeding up journeys.'

Route One website, 3 July 2018

* * *

India bus crash: More than 40 dead in northern Uttarakhand state

More than 40 people have died when a bus fell into a gorge in a mountainous region of northern India.

The incident on Sunday occurred in Nanidhanda area of Pauri Garhwal district in the state Uttarakhand.

'The bus lost control and swerved off the road, into a deep valley. It broke into two pieces on impact and it is now in a small river at the bottom of the valley,' disaster management official Deepesh Chandra Kala told AFP news agency.

'As per official records, 45 people are dead, while many are injured,' Surendra Agrawal, official at the Chief Minister's Office in Uttarakhand told Al Jazeera.

'Over 50 people were travelling in the bus,' he added. 'A probe will determine the reason of the accident, it could be human error or a technical snag.'

Prime Minister Narendra Modi's office tweeted that Modi was 'extremely saddened' by the news of the deaths.

Road accidents are frequent in India, with uncontrolled traffic junctions, badly maintained vehicles, and poor driving standards blamed for most incidents. ... A person is killed in a road accident every four minutes, according to government data. ... About 1.2 million Indians were killed in car accidents between 2004-2014, while 5.5 million were seriously injured.

Al Jazeera, 1 July 2018

7
When the Dust Settles

16 July 2018

EXPRESSIONS OF devotion and gratitude to Gareth Southgate took various forms in the heady World Cup summer of 2018. In Lichfield, Staffordshire an 18-year-old logistics apprentice called Alex Allan Smith decided that if England reached the semi-final he would get, on his left buttock, a tattoo of Gareth Southgate's face and the words 'It's coming home'. Soon afterwards, before the quarter-final against Sweden, while on holiday in Magaluf, his friend Sam asked: 'Why don't you just get it now?' They had a few drinks and tossed a coin. 'I got tails,' Alex told the *Wolverhampton Express & Star*, 'so I went straight up to the tattoo parlour to do it. My friends were laughing, they couldn't believe it. All of them liked it though. I definitely think England will win. I don't think I will regret the tattoo.' Let's hope not.

Alex was not the only Englishman to decorate his body with devotional art. Tattoo parlours in Walsall had requests for a St George's flag, Three Lions badges, the words 'England till I die', and 'It's coming home'. In Leeds, a 32-year-old carpet fitter called Jamie Richardson had a picture of the trophy and 'England 2018 World Cup Winners' tattooed on his stomach. He said he'd had a premonition when England were leading Panama 5-0 at half-time in a group game that they'd go on to win the competition. 'I thought if I get that tattoo then football will come home,' he told the *Yorkshire Evening Post*. 'When the dust settles and the World Cup is on the plane home, I'll be able to say that I always believed when others said we would be knocked out.' Getting the tattoo, he said, was a patriotic act. 'England expects every fan to do their duty. It's bigger than football – we're English – we're proud and we're better than everyone else.'

London staged a more visible act of homage. On 16 July, after England lost the third-place play-off match, Southgate tube station, at the northern end of the Piccadilly Line, was temporarily renamed Gareth Southgate tube station. It was all done quite formally with the words 'Gareth Southgate' replacing traditional signage at the front of the art deco building, and big red, white and blue 'Gareth Southgate' roundels on the west and east platforms. One sign read: 'Thanks Gareth for the incredible journey. Southgate is yours.'

Geoff Marshall, an indefatigable chronicler of public transport in London, posted a video of his visit to the station and his meeting with a happy, flag-waving lady called Tammy. She'd made a special trip to Gareth Southgate 'because we're all so proud of the England football team and how well they've done this year. … It came home! The spirit! And we're so proud!' A teenage girl, wearing an identical red football t-shirt and holding a rolled-up flag, stood a few feet away looking uncertain. The station renaming was only supposed to last two days, but Tammy reckoned it should be permanent: 'I have friends who go mad if I even mention the word football and this year they've been sitting there *watching it*! The public have proper reconnected their love for football, and it's only because of this man!'

* * *

Trump sides with Russia against FBI at Helsinki summit

US President Donald Trump has defended Russia over claims of interference in the 2016 presidential election. After face-to-face talks with Russian President Vladimir Putin, Mr Trump contradicted US intelligence agencies and said there had been no reason for Russia to meddle in the vote.

Mr Putin reiterated that Russia had never interfered in US affairs. The two men held nearly two hours of closed-door talks in the Finnish capital Helsinki on Monday.

BBC News, 16 July 2018

* * *

Obama warns of uncertain times in Mandela tribute

Former US President Barack Obama delivered the annual Nelson Mandela Lecture in Johannesburg on Tuesday, using the first major speech since leaving the White House to honor the late South African leader on what would have been his 100th birthday.

In a wide-ranging talk, Obama decried 'reactionary' and 'strongman' politics, while calling for wider respect for the rights of women and an independent media.

With a thinly veiled reference to his successor, Donald Trump, Obama opened by remarking on the 'strange and uncertain times we are in ... and they are very strange.' The ex-president noted that in a moment filled with 'disturbing headlines,' it was imperative to 'get some perspective.'

'More than a quarter century after Madiba walked out of prison, I still have to stand here saying people of all races and women and men are the same,' Obama said, referencing Nelson Mandela's clan name.

In a speech characterized by its impassioned defense of equality across race, gender, sexual orientation and national lines, Obama slammed the 'small-minded' nature of 'politics of fear, resentment and retrenchment,' without naming any specific politicians.

In what was perhaps another allusion to Trump, he criticized leaders who 'just make stuff up ... when they're caught in a lie and they just double down.' ... 'Those in power seek to undermine every institution ... that gives democracy meaning,' including the free press, the former leader said. He added a stern warning: 'I am not being alarmist. I am simply stating the facts. Look around.'

The 14,000 people who came to see Obama speak in Johannesburg regularly broke out into thunderous applause throughout the talk.

Deutsche Welle, 17 July 2018

* * *

A video showing a woman tearing down a Tube sign at Gareth Southgate station has sparked outrage among football fans.

Transport for London (TfL) announced earlier this week it would be renaming the station in honour of the England manager for 48 hours after the Three Lions' efforts at the World Cup. Although the sign was due to come down last night, a TfL spokesman confirmed the woman was not a Tube staff member and did not have permission to carry out the act. ...

Many people took to Twitter in anger after the video emerged. One person described the woman's behaviour as 'shocking', while another added: 'Southgate we still love you.' Another Twitter user called the incident 'totally bang out of order', with a different social media user adding: 'Poor form all round.'

***Evening Standard*, 20 July 2018**

8
Purgatory

Winter/Spring 2020

TWO ASSASSINS are standing in front of what, with hindsight, can be read as a representation of the state of football during Covid. It's a three-panelled painting, executed in oil on wood, and its symbolism is disturbing and obscure. In the top right corner, we see a blazing castle. To the left and lower down, a myriad of nightmares: a giant knife, a colossal rat, an inhuman-scale church bell, sinister-looking ladders, multiple corpses, a shoe with a sail, a creature with a human face and lizard body, a sword-pierced naked man wearing a helmet and riding a cow. A detail seldom noted by art historians is that this helmet resembles a shiny ball and it has a cockerel on top.

The triptych, attributed to Hieronymus Bosch, is called 'The Last Judgement', and, as you probably guessed, we are in a museum in Bruges in *In Bruges*. It's the scene where the film's hitmen muse mournfully on the afterlife. The painting, says Brendan Gleeson's character, represents 'the final day on Earth, when mankind will be judged for the crimes they've committed'. Post-death options seem to be Heaven, Hell or Purgatory. And what's Purgatory? Oh, that's 'the in-betweeny one', says Colin Farrell. It means 'you weren't really shit, but you weren't all that great either. Like Tottenham.'

Football in early 2021 felt distinctly in-betweeny: not all that great, but better than the year before. Confounding medieval theology, the game in 2020 entered hell, survived by hurling itself into limbo, yet never stopped dreaming of a return to its former condition that, for all its faults and foibles, came to seem rather heavenly.

In December 2019, shortly after Boris Johnson's Tories crushed Jeremy Corbyn's Labour in the British general election, a strange new disease emerged in China. By the following month it had spread, initially to Thailand. By February the Covid virus was in Europe, with northern Italy first, probably due to its trade links with China. On 19 February Atalanta of Bergamo played a Champions League match against Valencia. Because Atalanta's stadium wasn't large enough, the biggest game in the club's history was played in Milan and their fans were ecstatic when they won 4-1. They had no way of knowing Death enjoyed the match as much as they did. Soon, thousands of Atalanta supporters, their friends and families were falling sick, and many were dying. Crammed together on the fatal day in buses, trains, the shiny Milan metro, and in the San Siro stadium (not to mention bars and homes back in Bergamo, the fans had unwittingly taken part in a 'super-spreader event'. Soon northern Italy was the European epicentre of the disease: hospitals, coffin-makers and cemeteries were overwhelmed; convoys of military vehicles collected bodies for cremation elsewhere.

Forewarned by these horrors, Britain had precious extra weeks to prepare – and failed to do so. As Lady Hallett's Covid inquiry later discovered, the government hadn't adequately planned or prepared for years and, when the pandemic struck, was initially more interested in Brexit (the UK formally left the EU at the end of January) than in the emerging health disaster.

In her book *Breathtaking*, the hospice doctor Rachel Clarke, who fell ill with the disease in its first weeks and later chronicled its effects across the NHS, wrote that on 26 February one of the country's foremost epidemiologists, Professor John Edmunds, warned a government committee that if no action was taken to reduce infection rates, then 27 million Britons could be infected, and 380,000 people could die. He wasn't far wrong. Around the same time, a friend of mine in Rome whose sister was a minister in the Italian government told me Italy was warning every country – including Britain – that what was coming would be far worse than they anticipated.

On 9 March, former Tory minister Rory Stewart urged the UK government to close schools, cancel medium and large gatherings, and test all passengers coming into the country from Covid hotspots. 'There is no justification for half-hearted measures,' he said. 'The government and the mayor [of London] keep saying they are simply following "scientific advice". But the scientists are clear that this is now a political decision – on whether the government are prepared to spend very serious sums of money, and take a large economic hit, to maximise protection of the population.'

They were not, but other European countries were acting. On 23 February, Italy quarantined 11 northern towns. The entire country went into full lockdown on 9 March. Yet three weeks after what was now understood to have been the calamity of Atalanta v Valencia, the UK government allowed two sporting super-spreader events to go ahead: the Liverpool v Atletico Madrid match at Anfield on 11 March and the Cheltenham Festival, where more than 250,000 people gathered between 10 and 13 March.

My last social outing was on 5 March. We didn't yet appreciate that the virus was airborne; we thought it was passed by touch, so we awkwardly elbow-bumped and felt vaguely fearful. The next day I decided to isolate.

On 23 March, Prime Minister Boris Johnson belatedly ordered a national lockdown. We didn't know that his initial response had been informed by the misguided concept of 'herd immunity'. The idea was that if you let the virus rip through the population, most people would catch it, survive and thereby gain immunity. Scientists soon realised this was a crazy idea as survivors could be reinfected, many would be maimed by Long Covid and the overall death toll would be far higher than if protective measures were adopted. We didn't know either that later in the year the *Daily Mail* would report Johnson as saying: 'No more fucking lockdowns – let the bodies pile high in their thousands.' Nor that the policy (later ruled 'unlawful') of sending untested hospital patients into care homes would kill almost 20,000 people in three months. Eventually, when news of Johnson and his ministers' incompetence, corruption and lockdown parties was revealed, he and his party would be doomed politically. But for months, as Labour struggled with the legacy of Corbyn, and new opposition leader Keir Starmer failed to make much impact, the Tories rode high, especially when vaccines arrived to begin to rescue us.

Meanwhile, Covid lockdowns and restrictions played havoc with sport. Elite football stopped entirely in England on 13 March 2020. In April,

Gareth Southgate voluntarily took a 30 per cent pay cut, and health secretary Matt Hancock politicised the issue by telling Premier League footballers to 'play their part' in the crisis by taking pay cuts too (most did, some didn't, while some clubs furloughed non-playing staff). Soon, the only football being played anywhere in the world was in Belarus, and watching YouTube coverage of teams like Sputnik Rechitsa and Torpedo Zhodino became a thing. Channel 4's screening of Asif Kapadia's great documentary about Maradona at the end of March 2020 became a major event.

And then we entered the peculiar half-light period of Purgatory. Lockdown was partially eased, and football resumed under strict medical supervision in empty stadiums watched by TV cameras with fake crowd noise to cover the eerie silence. In the autumn a second Covid wave arrived and with it another belated national lockdown in November. That was partially lifted in December (socially distanced crowds of up to 2,000 were briefly allowed at some football matches) then reintroduced in January. Only in May 2021, as Gareth Southgate prepared for the delayed Euro

2020 tournament, did a move back to the old normality begin in earnest.

* * *

Castle on fire

Lake Buena Vista, Fla.– Reedy Creek fire officials say a small fire at Walt Disney World's Magic Kingdom Tuesday may have sprouted from a tree.

WESH-TV reports that officials say the fire near Cinderella Castle could have been caused by debris from the classic fireworks show set off at the castle.

The castle and surrounding areas were evacuated. Firefighters quickly extinguished the flames.

Associated Press, 15 December 2021

* * *

Boris Johnson wants to remain as Prime Minister for another decade so he serves 'longer than Thatcher'.

The incendiary claim came after Mr Johnson made one of his biggest gambles in office, introducing a new National Insurance levy to fund social care. From April next year National Insurance will rise 1.25 per cent, to fund NHS spending and an £86,000 cap on individual social care payments.

Speaking to *The Times* a cabinet minister claimed Mr Johnson wants to be Prime Minister for 'longer than Thatcher', who held the post between 1979 and 1990.

They said: 'Boris will want to go on and on. The stuff Dom [Cummings] was saying about him going off into the sunset was nonsense. He's very competitive. He wants to go on for longer than Thatcher.'

In June Dominic Cummings, formerly Mr Johnson's chief advisor, said the Prime Minister had a 'clear plan' to quit two years after the next general election, expected in 2023 or 2024. He argued Mr Johnson wants to be 'making money' and having fun, rather than trying to stay at 10 Downing Street for the long-term.

***Daily Express*, 11 September 2021**

* * *

Sir Keir Starmer has admitted he considered quitting as Labour leader after the party lost both the Hartlepool by-election and council seats in 2021.

Speaking to Sky News political editor Beth Rigby ahead of tomorrow's contests, Sir Keir called it 'a low point', with his party recording a net loss of eight councils, as well as the North East constituency - which had been held by Labour since the 1970s, but went to the Conservatives on the night.

'I did [consider quitting] because I didn't feel that I should be bigger than the party and that if I couldn't bring about the change, perhaps there should be a change,' he said.

'But actually, in the end, I reflected on it, talked to very many people and doubled down and determined, no, it is the change in the Labour Party we need.'

Sir Keir said he felt 'vindicated' by his decision to stay on 'because we are now a changed party, nobody argues with that'.

Sky News, 1 May 2024

9
Knees

6 June 2021

IT WAS Gareth's finest hour. Long after the football is forgotten, it might become the best-remembered part of his legacy. Alternatively, the football could be revered and the other stuff ignored. You just never know how the future will remember its past.

I'm talking, of course, about Gareth's role in the great wave of symbolic anti-racism knee-taking inspired by the Black Lives Matter protests that followed the murder of George Floyd in America in May 2020. Floyd, a 46-year-old Black man, was killed by a white policeman called Derek Chauvin. American police had been brutalising and killing innocent Black men for decades, but this crime was caught on video. For nine terrible minutes Chauvin pressed his knee into Floyd's neck as he struggled to breathe. People around the world were horrified. Protests erupted everywhere, and when English club football restarted after the Covid lockdown a few weeks later, the killing inspired players at Premier League and Championship clubs to take the knee to protest against racism in and around the game.

Pretty much everyone in English football was on board. The Premier League even temporarily mandated players' names on their shirts be replaced by the words 'Black Lives Matter', though this stopped when BLM was linked to more contentious matters such as toppling a statue in Bristol of slave trader Edward Colston, or the campaign to 'defund the police'. Nevertheless, in the months that followed, in stadiums still empty of fans because of Covid, footballers taking the knee protest against racism became routine. By the following summer, as the Euros of 2021 drew near, the players of the national team, fed up with racist abuse, decided to take the knee too.

You'd think this would have been uncontroversial. After all, who in their right minds would be in favour of racism? At the beginning of

June, at the Riverside in Middlesbrough, before England's warm-up games against Austria and Romania, we found out: people in their far-right minds would. Some of the socially distanced fans allowed into the stadium on those two nights noisily booed the knee-takers, though many others applauded. Various right-wing politicians and commentators jumped in. MP Lee Anderson (soon to be deputy chairman of the Tory Party) said he would boycott 'my beloved England team' if the knee-taking continued. Another Tory MP, Brendan Clarke-Smith, denounced the kneeling as a 'ridiculous empty gesture'.

As tensions rose, Prime Minister Boris Johnson made his intervention: he refused to condemn those doing the booing. The day after the Romania match, his spokesperson said the Prime Minister 'fully respects the right of those who choose to peacefully protest and make their feelings known', adding: 'On taking the knee, specifically, the Prime Minister is more focused on action rather than gestures.' A week later the Home Secretary Priti Patel told GB News that if fans were booing, then 'that was a choice for them, quite frankly'. As to the kneeling footballers: 'I just don't support people participating in that type of gesture politics.' Meanwhile, on the day of George Floyd's funeral in Texas, which took place three days after the Romania game, Labour leader Keir Starmer released a photo of himself and his deputy Angela Rayner knee-taking in his office. The matter had become party political.

Traditionally, England managers have kept clear of any contentious issues. But Gareth – fully backed by the FA – was adamant. Before the Austria game, he said: 'We are totally united on it, we are totally committed to supporting each other … We feel, more than ever, determined to take the knee through this tournament. We accept that there might be an adverse reaction; we are just going to ignore that and move forward.' After the match he commented: 'I was pleased [the booing] was drowned out by the majority of the crowd, but I can't deny that it happened. Some people seem to think it's a political stand and they don't agree with it. But that's not the reason the players are doing it.'

As England's first match in the tournament, against Croatia, approached, he became even firmer: he and the players would not be deflected.

He refused to answer any more questions on the subject. The stance seemed to work. The FA urged England fans to support the gesture, which it said was not 'aligned to a political organisation' but an act of 'unity and fighting against inequality'. Against Croatia a few fans at Wembley did boo, but they were drowned out. The pattern was repeated in subsequent matches and soon died away.

How decisive was Gareth's stand? Reflecting on it three years later in an episode of the *Heroes & Humans of Football* podcast, Mehreen Khan, economics editor of *The Times*, gave most of the credit to the team's Black players, especially Marcus Rashford and Tyrone Mings, who had blasted Boris Johnson's interventions. Contrariwise, her co-host Simon Kuper was full of praise for the way Southgate – 'this older white guy' – had stood up to the attacks from the right. 'He defends his team very vocally and he says, "Look, I'm trying to learn what it means to be a young Black man in England to be discriminated against, to be at risk of police violence and I think you should all try and put yourself in their shoes and try and empathise." This is a country where the England manager had never in my experience taken a stance on any social issue and Southgate says, "No, I'm going to talk about society."'

As a thought experiment, we can wonder how Gareth's predecessors would have reacted. In particular, what would his immediate predecessor, Brexit-voting Sam Allardyce, have done? Judging by his public pronouncements, it may well have been much the same. Interviewed during the tournament, Allardyce said it was 'very important' for England players to kneel before matches, and they should continue to campaign against racism: 'This is obviously something that's gone on for many, many months now and we tend to do that in support of Black Lives Matter ... Irrespective of what other people think or what other people may do', it was 'very important' for football to try 'to make a stand.'

But there's one thing Big Sam would not have done. He would not have sat down and written a soon-to-be-legendary letter to the nation.

* * *

Scotland midfielder Kenny McLean has been left 'absolutely devastated' by a knee ligament injury that rules him out of this summer's Euro 2020 finals.

The 29-year-old will miss the next 12 weeks after he was injured in Norwich City's 2-2 final-day Championship draw with Barnsley on Saturday. McLean has 'significant damage' to the right-side medial collateral ligament.

'Lots of hard work to come and I'll be supporting the lads from afar,' he said on Twitter.

BBC Sport, 11 May 2021

* * *

Liverpool centre-back Virgil van Dijk has ruled himself out of Euro 2020 to concentrate on recovering from his knee injury in time for the start of the new Premier League season. The 29-year-old is captain of the Netherlands national team, but will not be leading his side this summer as he completes his recovery from a ligament injury in the Merseyside derby in October 2020 and has missed the majority of the campaign as a result.

Club manager Jurgen Klopp had previously been non-committal over whether he would return to play a part in the current season, while his national team boss Frank de Boer insisted it would be Van Dijk's decision over whether or not to feature at the European Championship.

Independent, 12 May 2001

* * *

Zlatan Ibrahimovic will miss this summer's European Championship due to a knee injury. Ibrahimovic went off after suffering the injury in the 64th minute of AC Milan's 3-0 win against Juventus last week ... The forward has been recommended to undergo a cautious rehabilitation process that could last six weeks - which put his place at Euro 2020 in jeopardy.

His national side Sweden have confirmed that the 39-year-old informed head coach Janne Andersson that the injury has made him unavailable for this summer's tournament.

Milan have two games remaining in the Serie A season, while Sweden kick-off their Euro 2020 campaign against Spain on June 14.

***New York Times*, 15 May 2021**

10
Gettysburg

8 June 2021

IN JAMES Graham's play *Dear England*, sports psychologist Pippa Grange is the person who gives Gareth Southgate the idea to write the letter from which the play takes its name. We are deep into the second act and have reached early 2021. The Covid-delayed Euros will soon be upon Gareth, his players and the audience, and our hero is fretting about the burden on his team: 'It takes broad shoulders to carry a country's dreams.' When Pippa suggests he speaks directly to the nation, Gareth takes this to mean he use social media, and he'd 'rather eat [his] own face' than do that. 'Well, write to them then,' says Pippa, 'a letter to everyone, old school: "Dear England…".' Gareth tries out the words but decides, according to the stage direction, that they feel 'silly'. Eight script pages later, however, he changes his mind. Having just told his players to find *their* voices, he now, as played by Joseph Fiennes in the National Theatre production, finds his voice. The lights go down, he strides to a perfect spot at the front of the stage, stands in the spotlight and begins – in his no-longer-waistcoated, Garethy way – to orate.

The idea for what history calls the Gettysburg Address came from a local lawyer called David Wills. Local, that is, to the unimaginable carnage of the decisive battle of the American Civil War, which took place near his town in July 1863. The Battle of Gettysburg would have been more decisive if the Union commander had pursued the retreating Confederate army. To the disgust of President Abraham Lincoln, General Meade let Robert E. Lee's forces get away, staying instead to clear the 'debris' of the battle, described by historian Garry Wills (no relation) as 'mainly a matter of rotting horseflesh and manflesh – thousands of fermenting bodies, with gas-distended bellies, deliquescing in the July heat.' Four months later, with some of the remains still unsorted and unburied, thoughts turned to commemoration, and it fell to the redoubtable David Wills to organise a ceremony to consecrate a cemetery in one corner of the battlefield.

The main event would be a two-hour speech by renowned orator Edward Everett. Wills also asked President Lincoln to 'say a few remarks' just before the hymns and singing at the end. In the event, Lincoln's remarks – merely 268 words long and taking just over two minutes to deliver (barely longer than Gareth's 221-word speech in the play) – dwarfed their surroundings. Everett's epic was supposed to be the Gettysburg Address, but Lincoln proved size isn't anything. He made one of the greatest political speeches in the English language, up there with Churchill's war oratory and Martin Luther King's 'I Have a Dream'.

To be fair to the lad, Gareth Southgate wasn't trying to compete. He didn't even write a speech; it was James Graham who shortened it and made it a performance piece. Gareth's heartfelt 1,696-word open letter was published on the Players' Tribune website on 8 June 2016.

The letter is better than the speech in the play, and in some ways it parallels the Address. For a start, there's humility in both. 'The world will little note, nor long remember what we say here,' says the soon-to-be-murdered president. 'At home, I'm below the kids and the dogs in the pecking order,' says Gareth. And the context is similar in that both men spoke in the shadow of recent and continuing mass death. Some 50,000 men died at Gettysburg out of a total of 620,00 soldiers plus an uncounted number of civilians in the war. Just under 78,000 people died of Covid in England and Wales during 2021 out of a UK pandemic total of 227,000. Lincoln talked of 'the brave men, living and dead, who struggled here'. Southgate hymns his 'special group' of players ('humble, proud and liberated in being their true selves') but stresses the proximity of suffering: 'Everyone in this country has been directly affected by isolation and loss. But we have also seen countless examples of heroism and sacrifice. It's given us all a new understanding of the fragility of life and what really matters.'

Compared with the soaring power of Lincoln's extraordinary finale, Gareth's climax feels leaden: 'Of course, I know my players and I will be judged on winning matches. Believe me. But the reality is that the result is just a small part. It's about how we conduct ourselves. And how we bring people together. That lasts beyond the summer. That lasts forever.' Lincoln's went: 'From these honored dead we take increased devotion to that cause for which they gave the last full measure of devotion – that we here highly resolve that these dead shall not have died in vain – that this nation, under God, shall have a new birth of freedom – and that government of the people, by the people, for the people, shall not perish from the earth.' But, like the president, Gareth articulated something bold and new: a picture of his nation rooted in the idea of equality. Football managers don't usually venture into such territory.

Lincoln had claimed 'Four score and seven years ago our fathers brought forth on this continent a new nation, conceived in liberty, and dedicated to the proposition that all men are created equal. Now we are engaged in a great civil war, testing whether that nation, or any nation so conceived and so dedicated, can long endure.' Southgate fuses his old-school idea of Englishness, derived from his beloved grandfather ('Queen and country', royal pageantry, 'affinity for the military and service in the name of your country'), with a new but equally valid Englishness represented by his ethnically diverse squad.

Speaking to the younger generation, he wrote: 'Your notion of Englishness is quite different from my own. I understand that, too. I understand that on this island, we have a desire to protect our values and traditions – as we should – but that shouldn't come at the expense of introspection and progress. Regardless of your upbringing and politics, what is clear is that we are an incredible nation – relative to our size and population – that has contributed so much to the arts, science and sport. We do have a special identity and that remains a powerful motivator.'

As Julian Coman observed in *The Guardian*, Gareth was making 'an unashamedly patriotic case for a more inclusive country. The themes of time, nationhood, pride and collective experience – rather than an abstract assertion of universal rights – are the channels through which his argument flows, linking the postwar generations. From memories of his grandfather to recollections of watching the England football team as a boy, to the journeys of his own players from often humble beginnings, the letter chronicles the interweaving of individual biographies with the bigger national story over time.' Sensitivity to the past allowed 'the traditionalist Southgate to be so persuasive and radical when he talks about the future'.

James Graham's truncated version doesn't bring out this aspect. He doesn't even quote Gareth's rebuke to those who 'choose to insult somebody for something as ridiculous as the colour of their skin'. 'You're on the losing side. It's clear to me that we are heading for a much more tolerant and understanding society, and I know our lads will be a big part of that. It might not feel like it at times, but it's true … I am confident that young kids of today will grow up baffled by old attitudes and ways of thinking.'

In an article based on his book *Lincoln at Gettysburg*, historian Garry Wills explains how Lincoln's speech subtly rewrote the United States' founding document. The Constitution had been about many things but was not primarily 'dedicated to the proposition that all men are created equal', as the Address has it. And the Civil War didn't start as a war against slavery. In its first two years, the North mostly thought it was fighting to preserve the Union. As Garry Wills puts it:

> Lincoln was [at Gettysburg] to clear the infected atmosphere of American history itself, tainted with official sins and inherited guilt. He would cleanse the Constitution … He altered the document from within, by appeal from its letter to the spirit, subtly changing the recalcitrant stuff of that legal compromise, bringing it to its own indictment. By implicitly doing this, he performed one of the most daring acts of open-air sleight of hand ever witnessed by the unsuspecting. Everyone in that vast throng of thousands was having his or her intellectual pocket picked. The crowd departed with a new thing in its ideological luggage, the new Constitution Lincoln had substituted for the one they had brought there with them … Lincoln had revolutionized the Revolution, giving people

a new past to live with that would change
their future indefinitely.

Not every American liked this new direction. Lincoln's murderer, John Wilkes Booth, was one. And the Civil War, though it destroyed the Confederacy and ended slavery in the South, fell well short of erasing racism. Today, 160 years on, one of history's nastiest ironies is that the Republican Party of Abraham Lincoln has become little more than a fascist personality cult for Donald Trump. Yet in deep ways Lincoln's speech did redefine America. It's too early to tell if Gareth's attempt will do the same for England.

* * *

Church books for Lent

Chapman's Sermons

Instruction and Encouragement for Lent - by Hobart

Readings for Every Day in Lent - by Sewell

Practical Directions for Lent

Southgate's Sermons

***Buffalo Daily Republic*, 28 March 1860**

The assassination of President Lincoln

Too dreadful to believe without the strongest evidence, but forcing itself upon us in spite of inclination, comes the appalling news of the assassination of the beloved President of the United States, and of the attempted murder of the respected head of the State Department of the nation. The whole loyal population mourns, and all those in rebellion should mourn. The first have lost a Chief Magistrate elected by their suffrages, by virtue of rare merits, of honesty, faithfulness, and unswerving devotion to the high duties of his responsible office. The disloyal class are deprived of a friend who has always plead their cause, and extended to them such clemency as is rare among rulers towards subjects in rebellion.

***Savannah Daily Herald*, 19 April 1865**

* * *

The public mind requires the consolations of Christian sympathy. There are, also, lessons, deep religious lessons, to be drawn from this universal bereavement ... For, although the blows which have so deeply wounded our peace were struck by wicked men, the lowest theory of Divine Providence must acknowledge that they fell, not only with the prescience, but with the permission of Deity.

–The Death of Lincoln, April 15th, 1865. Some of the religious lessons which it teaches.

A sermon, preached in Zion Church, New York, 23 April 1865, by the Rector, the Right Rev. Horatio Southgate

* * *

Four score and seven years ago our fathers brought forth on this continent, a new nation, conceived in Liberty, and dedicated to the proposition that all men are created equal.

Now we are engaged in a great civil war, testing whether that nation, or any nation so conceived and so dedicated, can long endure. We are met on a great battle-field of that war. We have come to dedicate a portion of that field as a final resting place for those who here gave their lives that that nation might live. It is altogether fitting and proper that we should do this.

But, in a larger sense, we cannot dedicate, we cannot consecrate, we cannot hallow this ground. The brave men, living and dead, who struggled here have consecrated it, far above our poor power to add or detract. The world will little note, nor long remember what we say here, but it can never forget what they did here. It is for us the living, rather, to be dedicated here to the unfinished work which they who fought here have thus far so nobly advanced. It is rather for us to be here dedicated to the great task remaining before us, that from these honored dead we take increased devotion to that cause for which they gave the last full measure of devotion, that we here highly resolve that these dead shall not have died in vain, that this nation, under God, shall have a new birth of freedom, and that government of the people, by the people, for the people, shall not perish from the earth.

Abraham Lincoln, 19 November 1863

11
The Old Empire

17 June 2021

'DECLAN! DECLAN!' 'Rashford! Rashford! Marcus Rashford!' We can't see much. Just the team bus, a beefily masked security guy in a suit facing the small crowd, and a flight of steps to the side entrance of the hotel, which is partly hidden by shrubs. Unlike the animals who boarded Noah's ark, England's footballers, one by one, daintily climb the steps into the Marriott Maida Vale. That's what the hotel calls itself. And I can understand why estate agents and hoteliers might wish to brand it that way. But seeing as the hotel was built on the site of an Edwardian entertainment palace called the Kilburn Empire Music Hall and Theatre of Varieties; and the name of this street is Kilburn Priory (medieval nuns lived here!); and the hotel is opposite the Kilburn Gate housing estate; and Kilburn Library, Kilburn High Road overground station, and Kilburn branches of Tesco and Starbucks are all within a hundred yards ... well, locals like me consider this to be not really Maida Vale.

So much for place. What about the time? We seem to be a few hours from the Euro 2020 England v Scotland game in June 2021. The match will take place at Wembley, which is six miles away, up the old Roman road of which Kilburn High Road is a part, then turn left on to the North Circular. Alternatively, the England bus could drive up Willesden Lane past the cemetery where England's tragic first football captain is buried: Cuthbert Ottaway danced all night, caught a chill and died at the age of 27. Alternatively alternatively, the bus might wend through Dollis Hill and pass the house where *Hellraiser* was filmed. There are many routes to the great hereafter.

It's not easy to identify the football superstars as they flit up the steps. The quality of the video shot by a local resident isn't great, and the players wear Covid masks. Fortunately, the fans seem to know who's who. And what's what, because the mood is a mixture of delight and grievance. Amid occasional cheers, a woman's voice is heard: 'Wave!' she demands, '*Wave!!*' Most of the players are not waving. 'Oh, come on! *Come on!*' An old-fashioned male voice shouts 'Come on, England!' in a rattles-on-terraces kind of way, but the angry modern fan isn't buying it. 'When the England football team are being so rude that they can't even wave to their fans...' (she lets the unfinished accusation hang in the air) 'can't *even* wave to your fans? Can't even have a *wave* or something? Know what I mean? *D'you know* what I mean?" Phil Foden appears. At least it could be Phil. Masked and wearing a back-to-front baseball cap, he half turns as he ascends the steps, acknowledges the crowd, and earns a cheer. There's no mistaking Kalvin Phillips, though. Not with that hair. 'Kalvin! Kalvin! Come on, Kalvin!' goes the crowd. Someone explains: 'That's Kevin Phillips.'

It's hardly the first time important and famous people have graced the area. Frank Sinatra, the Beatles, the Stones, Bowie, Louis Armstrong and George Formby all played the Gaumont State, up the road. In grand, long-vanished houses just around the corner from the Empire, A.A. Milne spent his childhood, H.G. Wells taught, and George Orwell wrote *Animal Farm*. Across the street from Orwell lived the man who designed the Mount Rushmore monument. Just around another corner Victorian wizard William Friese-Greene supposedly invented cinema.

Yet I found myself inexplicably and deeply chuffed that England chose to spend some of their downtime ten minutes' walk from my flat. Inner and outer London is full of fancy and luxurious hotels but, of all the gin joints in all the towns in Zone 2, the team booked into mine. I loved the way excited fans gathered outside the Marriott. I saw them when I walked down the High Road. Sadly, the fun didn't last. Possibly because some idiots let off fireworks one night, for the semi-final and final England chose their more secluded, sylvan base, St George's Park, near Derby, and drove the 130 miles to Wembley, avoiding Kilburn entirely.

The slender local connection reminded me of an incident not far away but long ago. On the morning of the 1966 World Cup Final, to take their minds off the afternoon's game, Bobby Charlton left the England team base, the now-demolished Hendon Hall Hotel, and walked to my old neighbourhood with team-mate Ray Wilson to do some shopping. Ray bought a pair of shoes, Bobby some cufflinks. If I'd gone out that morning, I might have run into the legendary England men on the brink of their greatest triumph, though I doubt I'd have asked for a wave. When I remember 1966, I often think of that near-miss.

And what does any of this have to do with Gareth Southgate? Well, it has to do with popular history and collective memory. And those things are at the core of the 'Dear England' letter he wrote to fans before the tournament: 'There's something I tell our players before every England game,' he said. 'I really believe it with all my heart. I tell them that when you go out there, in this shirt, you have the opportunity to produce moments that people will remember forever. You are a part of an experience that lasts in the collective consciousness of our country.'

It's a lovely sentiment, but notice the boundaries Gareth draws: what matters, he reckons, are the moments people see 'out there', meaning on the pitch. Not behind the scenes or off-stage. Attenuated encounters mediated by security guards outside hotels are probably excluded. The letter also notes that 'footballers aren't as accessible to fans as they once were' but they have 'a duty' to 'interact with the public on matters such as equality, inclusivity and racial injustice'.

But memory and popular history don't work like that. It's not just matches that shape thoughts and feelings. And 'equality, inclusivity and racial injustice' aren't the only subjects fans might wish to talk about. Meaningful experiences tend to be more jagged, tangential, personal.

That line about 'collective consciousness' is striking too. It sounds close to Jung's idea of the collective *un*conscious, that storehouse of experience and impulses common to humanity of which individuals are unaware but which shape us and our societies. Did Gareth mean something like that? Probably not. Might the sheer strangeness of England-in-NW6 be linked to the related concept of 'archetypes'? Probably not that, either. More simply, I guess I'm just enchanted by the idea that the national team's Kilburn sojourn may one day be the stuff of folk memory. Reveries about it will last into the night, most likely around log fires. Stories will be told, songs sung, toasts drunk with mead. 'England stayed here once,' they'll say. 'And you know what? They never even fucking give us a wave.'

* * *

Biden warns of 'devastating' consequences for Russia if Navalny dies in prison

President Joe Biden said he warned Russian President Vladimir Putin Wednesday of consequences if jailed Russian opposition leader Alexey Navalny were to die in prison, though he declined to specify which actions he would take. 'I made it clear to him that I believe the consequences of that would be devastating for Russia,' Biden said. ...

Biden, who has posed autocracy versus democracy as a central theme of this moment, suggested he raised human rights extensively with Putin during the Geneva summit. 'I also told him that no president of the United States could keep faith with the American people if they did not speak out to defend our democratic values, to stand up for the universal and fundamental freedoms that all men and women have in our view,' he said.

CNN, 17 June 2021

* * *

Scottish fans arrive in London

Thousands of Scots descended on London yesterday ahead of tonight's crucial match against the Auld Enemy. Having lost their Euro 2020 opener to the Czech Republic, while England notched up a win over Croatia, Scotland need to take something from the game. But the Tartan Army were at their confident best as they arrived in the capital singing Scotland's anthem for the tournament, 'Yes sir, I can boogie'.

Fans arrived in waves of blue, kitted out in tartan hats, kilts and Scotland flags, creating a buoyant atmosphere ahead of the Wembley clash in front of a crowd of more than 20,000. Among them will be 25 members of the North of Scotland

Tartan Army supporters' club. Member Alan Duncan said: 'England are not as good as they are made out to be. I think we can get something out of the game at Wembley.'

On arrival in London some supporters criticised the lack of fan zone space available because of Covid-19 regulations. They gathered outside King's Cross train station, dancing and singing, but the traditional Scottish meeting spot of Trafalgar Square will not be accessible to them. Instead, it will be used as a socially-distanced, ticketed fan zone for 750 key workers, and the screen will not be visible without access.

***Press & Journal, Dundee*, 17 June 2021**

* * *

Kim Jong-un admits food shortages

North Korean leader Kim Jong-un has formally acknowledged that his country is facing food shortages. Addressing a meeting of senior leaders, Mr Kim said: 'The people's food situation is now getting tense.' He said the agricultural sector had failed to meet its grain targets due to typhoons last year, which caused flooding. ...

In April, Mr Kim made a rare admission of looming hardship, calling on officials to 'wage another, more difficult "Arduous March" in order to relieve our people of the difficulty, even a little'. The Arduous March is a term used by North Korea officials to refer to the country's struggle during the 1990s famine, when the fall of the Soviet Union left North Korea without crucial aid. The total number of North Koreans who starved to death at the time is not known, but estimates range up to three million.

BBC News, 17 June 2021

12
The One That Got Away

11 July 2021

'A REALLY difficult start for Italy,' says substitute Italian TV commentator Stefano Bizzotto, sounding stunned. *Difficile*? Not 'arf! We are two minutes into England's first major tournament final since 1966 and Luke Shaw has just swept us into the lead with the first attack. In the socially distanced VIP seats, seven-year-old Prince George celebrates adorably while his dad punches the air in grown-up triumph. Nearby, David Beckham does a discreet little fist-bump with his pal Tom Cruise. Almost everywhere else in the stadium, fans in white and red are leaping, prancing, hugging and screaming. Down at the front, a half-crazed man with no shirt cavorts with a flag. The cameras pick out the faces of Marco

Verratti and Gianluigi Donnarumma: the Italian players are in despair. Bizzotto, commentating for Italy's state broadcaster RAI because the usual guy has Covid, sounds as if he would rather be anywhere else in the world. Over the next couple of hours his mood will improve.

I'm writing this three years later, just after Gareth Southgate retired with his broken dream of winning a major trophy. In the aftermath of another lost Euro final, 2021 is being sentimentalised as 'the one that got away'. Gareth's other tournament near-misses certainly don't generate the same sense of 'if only'. In 2018, the nation was thrilled when his young and callow team reached the semi-final. They were outplayed there by the clever Croatians, but never mind; it was a joy while it lasted. In 2022, it was a pity Harry Kane missed his late penalty against France, but a narrow defeat to a strong team in a peculiar World Cup held at the wrong time of year did not plunge the nation into mourning. Even the loss to Spain a few days ago didn't feel too bad because Spain were obviously the better side. Against Italy back in 2021, though, with home advantage at a frenzied Wembley ... yeah, England coulda shoulda won that one. Watching the match again, free of the emotions of the time, the flaw in that argument becomes apparent.

England had played well through the tournament, drawing with Scotland but breezing past Croatia and Czechia in the group. Then came the cathartic, exhilarating 2-0 victory over Germany in the round of 16, England's first win in a major knockout match against that old enemy since 1966. Again, though, memory plays tricks. I remembered it as a one-sided affair, but actually it was tight, fierce and close. I'd mentally edited out the gnarly bits. Chances were few, Germany could have won, and Thomas Müller inexplicably missed a chance to equalise before Kane scored the killer second near the end.

Weak Ukraine were dispatched easily enough 4-0 in the quarter-final in Rome (England's only match away from Wembley), and Gareth's side were lucky to meet an exhausted Denmark in the semi-final. The Danes had recovered from and been inspired by the trauma of Christian Eriksen's near-death during a group match against Finland. Surfing a wave of relief, they'd gone on to be one of the teams of the tournament. At Wembley they were running on fumes but still good enough to take the lead and dominate for long periods before Harry Kane missed another late penalty to win the match for England in extra time (he scored the rebound).

With every victory, English euphoria grew and politicians tried to muscle in. Football was coming home (as in 1966, home advantage was proving handy) and Boris Johnson, so notable for his pre-tournament equivocation over the booing of England's knee-takers, posted preposterous pictures of himself in an England shirt with 'BORIS 10' printed on the back.

After days of mounting hype and hysteria, the perfect start to the final felt dreamlike and hallucinatory. A misunderstanding between goalkeeper Jordan Pickford and Harry Maguire gave the opposition a corner and, when England broke away, Italy seemed blind to the danger of the two wing-backs. (Were they wearing special temporary invisibility cloaks?) Kane found Kieran Trippier high on the right, and when he swung a long cross to the left Shaw seemed to materialise from nowhere to thump home a half-volley. *Incredibile!* Yet that was pretty much the end of the team's attacking ambition. Instead of going for the kill, England dropped back, sealed most routes to goal and concentrated on security. Big mistake. Big! Huge! As against Croatia three years before, surrendering the initiative was fatal. By the end of the first half, Italy had begun to dominate. In the second, their control became overwhelming. Leonardo Bonucci's scrappy equaliser on 67 minutes may have come from a corner, but the corner was the consequence of a 24-pass move that ended with a desperate Maguire clearance. As the move developed over a minute and a half, the increasingly nervous English crowd howled and booed, but their players were powerless to break Italy's rhythm. Official match stats later backed the impression that the only real football surprise that night was Italy not scoring again before winning the penalty shoot-out. England managed just 39 per cent possession and only six attempts on goal (and a couple of those were hopeless, from long range) compared to Italy's 20.

More significantly, off the field that day were some horrible non-football surprises. Racist abuse of the three England players who missed penalties

(Marcus Rashford, Jadon Sancho and Bukayo Saka) was shocking, but at least it inspired a gratifying and near-universal outpouring of love and support for the three, as well as prison sentences for some of their online abusers.

It was hard, though, to find any consolation for the appalling scenes in and around the stadium.

A few hours before the match I'd gone to Swiss Cottage for coffee with a friend. This involved travelling south on the Jubilee Line, which goes to Wembley Stadium. Most people were heading north, but my train was still full of drunk, belligerent, scary England fans. It reminded me of the worst days of the hooligan 1980s, and I walked home to avoid meeting them again. But my experience was nothing compared to what was happening around Wembley itself.

From early morning, thousands of ticketless fans, mostly drunk and/or coked up, started besieging the stadium and all but blocking Wembley Way. Police were slow to arrive, outnumbered and, for hours, overwhelmed. Initially, Wembley Way was chaotic but the mood was party-like. As kick-off drew closer, things turned nastier as hundreds of fans decided to punch their way past stewards, overthrow fences and jib, tailgate or force electronic gates to get inside the stadium. Five months later, Baroness Casey's independent report 'painted a terrifying picture in which fatalities and widespread injury were only narrowly avoided after authorities failed to plan for the "worst-case scenario" despite a series of warnings'. The disorder was a 'national shame'. Some two thousand fans without tickets had got inside. More threatening still, a mass of six thousand of them had stood like 'zombies' all through the match, waiting to charge past a thin line of riot police at the end if England won. Just as well in those circumstances that England did not win, and it started to rain, and the six thousand melted away. It was a miracle no one was killed.

* * *

'Irresponsible': UEFA slammed over Euro 2020 crowd numbers

German Minister of the Interior Horst Seehofer has called a decision by European football's governing body UEFA to allow big crowds at Euro

2020 'utterly irresponsible' especially given the spread of the Delta variant of the coronavirus. Seehofer told a news conference on Thursday that UEFA seems to have been driven by commercial considerations, which he said should not rank above health concerns.

Germany has permitted a limited number of fans into Munich's stadium but London's Wembley stadium had more than 40,000 for England's 2-0 win over the Germans in the last-16. 'I consider the position of UEFA to be absolutely irresponsible,' Seehofer said. 'We all know that contact avoidance and certain hygiene rules are indispensable to overcome infections.'

When you see pictures of 'people being very close to each other' and 'celebrating successes with big hugs', Seehofer added, it is 'preordained that this will promote the occurrence of infections'. On Wednesday, Karl Lauterbach, a health expert in the German parliament said: 'UEFA is responsible for the deaths of many people.'

Al Jazeera, 1 July 2021

* * *

Paul Mariner, former Ipswich and England striker, dies aged 68

The former Ipswich striker Paul Mariner, who in 1981 scored the goal that took England to their first World Cup finals since they lost as holders in 1970, has died at the age of 68. Mariner had had brain cancer. Mariner scored 139 goals in 339 games for Ipswich in a golden era in which they won the FA Cup in 1978 and Uefa Cup in 1981. His other clubs included Plymouth, Arsenal and Portsmouth, while he also earned 35 England caps and scored 13 times for his country.

PA Media, 10 July 2021

* * *

UK troop pullout could turn into a catastrophe for Afghans

Boris Johnson said of the withdrawal of the last British forces from Afghanistan that 3.6 million Afghan girls are now in school and women hold over a quarter of the seats in the parliament (Report, 9 July). Yes, but for how long? He said that we are safer because of everything the armed forces of Britain and many other countries have done. But many Afghans are not safer. We are, he said, not about to turn away. So how will we support Afghans if the Taliban retake Kabul?

I write as a doctor who has travelled many times to Afghanistan. Many of us in the UK share the great concerns of our Afghan colleagues: if this accelerated withdrawal is pursued without adequate military support from outside the country to the Afghan armed forces, there is a strong probability that the Taliban will prevail and much of the gains of the last 20 years will be lost. Even at this stage, we should take steps to prevent a hurried departure from turning into a catastrophe comparable to the US departure from Saigon.

Stewart Britten, Exeter

Letter to *The Guardian*, 11 July 2021

13
La Belle Équipe

10 December 2022

YET AGAIN, it wasn't quite the way I remembered. England were the better team. Balanced, powerful and coherent, they controlled the midfield for long periods and were probably good enough to have gone on and won the whole damned tournament. The 'fatal' penalty miss did not, as instant legend had it, come right at the end because the match went on for a further 16 minutes. And if it's any help (it isn't), and if you take xGs (the 'expected goals' metric) seriously (I'm not sure I do), you might almost say England even sort of morally won 2.59-1.32. Except they didn't. Anyway, the bottom line is this: losing that World Cup quarter-final was no one's fault, not even the Romans.

Watching the England 1 France 2 game in Qatar again, but this time with the French TV coverage, is a bittersweet revelation. In an unnecessarily long and intrusive half-time interview with his team already on the pitch, Didier Deschamps calls England a *belle équipe*. Later, he looks worried every time the cameras cut to him. Actually, Didier Deschamps usually looks worried when cameras cut to him, and he was probably just being polite. So scratch that. But captain/goalkeeper Hugo Lloris ('king of the air!' because he keeps grabbing high crosses) is France's best player: six excellent saves. Superstar Kylian Mbappé (key man when France won the World Cup in 2018 and destined to score three times in this year's final) barely gets a touch because Kyle Walker is *superbe*. And in the 77th minute the commentators are happily astonished when Olivier Giroud nearly scores, because it's one of France's few second-half chances. They're even happier a minute later when he scores the winning goal after a corner: the ball is cleared, then goes back to corner-taker Antoine Griezmann, who crosses for Giroud to head in via Harry Maguire's shoulder. Without the deflection, England's goalkeeper

Jordan Pickford might have saved it. It's a shame Harry Kane put his penalty over the bar because the French players later admitted England would likely have won in extra time, and they'd have been favourites to beat Morocco in the next match and may well have beaten Messi's Argentina in the final. For once, England had a proper 'if only'.

And it wasn't England's only good game that year. Unlike Gareth's other tournaments, they didn't play a single truly ropey match, the only slight blemish being the close-fought 0-0 with USA in the group. But they thumped Iran 6-2, and Wales 3-0, and sauntered past Senegal in the second round, again by 3-0.

In 2018 England reached the semi-final, then in 2020 (2021) and 2024 the final. But 2022 was probably Gareth's best tournament. When James Graham first pitched his idea for a play about Gareth, he learned that the FA were already working on what they called a 'three-act structure': build through World Cup 2018 and Euro 2020 then win in 2022. They nearly pulled it off.

* * *

Ukraine repels Russian offensive in eastern Ukraine, says General Staff

Units of Ukraine's Armed Forces repelled attacks by Russian invaders near 11 settlements in Luhansk and Donetsk oblasts, Ukraine's General Staff reported in their Dec. 11 morning update.

Ukrainian forces repelled enemy attacks near the settlements of Novoselivske, Andriyivka, Chervonopopivka, Zhytlivka, Serebryanske, and Bilohorivka in Luhansk Oblast, and Verkhnyokamyanske, Soledar, Bakhmutske, Pidhorodnye, and Bakhmut in Donetsk Oblast.

The enemy also launched three missiles and 17 air strikes, as well as more than 60 attacks from multiple rocket launchers.

Meanwhile, Ukrainian missile forces and artillery struck three enemy command posts and three troop, weapons, and material concentrations in the past 24 hours. Russia continues to shell Ukrainian settlements along the entire front line. The General Staff maintains that the threat of missile strikes on the energy and critical infrastructure objects throughout the territory of Ukraine still remains.

The New Voice of Ukraine, 11 December 2022

* * *

Putin's war 'could spin out of control', says NATO chief

The head of NATO expressed worry that the fighting in Ukraine could spin out of control and become a war between Russia and NATO, according to an interview released on Friday.

'If things go wrong, they can go horribly wrong,' NATO secretary-general Jens Stoltenberg said in remarks to Norwegian broadcaster NRK. 'It is a terrible war in Ukraine. It is also a war that can become a full-fledged war that spreads into a major war between NATO and Russia,' he said. 'We are working on that every day to avoid that.'

The Kremlin has repeatedly accused NATO allies of becoming party to the conflict by providing Ukraine with weapons, training its troops and feeding military intelligence to attack Russian forces.

Speaking on Friday via video link to defence and security chiefs of several ex-Soviet nations, Russian president Vladimir Putin again accused the West of using Ukraine as a tool against his country.

'For many years, the West shamelessly exploited and pumped out its resources, encouraged genocide and terror in the Donbas and effectively turned the country into a colony,' he said. 'Now it's cynically using the Ukrainian people as cannon fodder, as a ram against Russia by continuing to supply Ukraine with weapons and ammunition, sending mercenaries and pushing it to a suicidal track.'

Ukrainians say they are fighting against an unwanted invader and aggressor.

Heavy fighting continued yesterday, mostly in regions that Russia illegally annexed in September. Ukraine's presidential office said five civilians have been killed and another 13 wounded by Russian shelling in the last 24 hours.

***Irish Independent*, 10 December 2022**

* * *

Deschamps full of praise for 'underappreciated' England rival Southgate

France coach Didier Deschamps believes Gareth Southgate is underappreciated in England as he hailed his counterpart ahead of their World Cup quarter-final clash. ...

'I very much like Gareth,' Deschamps said on the eve of the game at Al Bayt Stadium.

'We have met on a number of occasions and have talked about a number of things. Not everyone appreciates him so much in his own country, that isn't because he wasn't a good footballer himself – he had a long and distinguished career and he is also a very good coach. He has enabled England to get some very good results over the years and I very much like him.'

***The Scotsman*, 10 December 2022**

* * *

Cat-ar 2022: England players to adopt 'Dave' the cat after leaving World Cup

England's footballers are coming home without the World Cup trophy but were not entirely empty-handed on leaving their training base in Al Wakrah on Sunday.

The defenders Kyle Walker and John Stones, who both started for Gareth Southgate's team in Saturday's 2-1 defeat by France, befriended a stray tabby cat during their four-week stay in Qatar.

Stones named their handsome new feline companion Dave, while Walker had said they planned to adopt the cat and bring him home to England should the Three Lions ultimately triumph.

Despite that dream again failing to become a reality, it seems the players had become too fond of Dave to say a final farewell when they departed Al Wakrah.

The cat was transported to a local veterinary clinic for tests and vaccinations and will spend four months in quarantine before what is presumably a free transfer to Manchester City – or to the care of Stones or Walker, who both play for the Premier League champions.

'They're still undecided as to who's having him but he's going back,' said a woman tasked with taking Dave to the vet's on Sunday, in a video posted by Rich McCarthy on Twitter.

'He was just there one day so we've just adopted him, me and Stonesy,' Walker told the

FA's official media channel during England's World Cup campaign. 'Dave is welcome to the table ... Some people really don't like the cat, but I love him.'

***The Guardian*, 11 December 2022**

14
Garlands

19–23 September 2022

IT WAS a week of farewells. On Monday, following ten days of official mourning, the nation buried Queen Elizabeth II. Barely had the haunting sound of the lone piper outside St George's Chapel in Windsor faded away than her box-fresh prime minister Liz Truss bade *arrivederci* to what was left of the UK's financial stability with a disastrous mini-budget. Chancellor Kwasi Kwarteng announced £45 billion of unfunded tax cuts to promote 'growth, growth, growth' and the pound collapsed. The gilt market went into freefall, mortgage costs soared, investors fled, and the Bank of England had to step in to save the nation's pension funds. To cap it all, in faraway Milan, Gareth Southgate's England took their leave of the top level of the Nations League by losing to Italy.

Pre-match formalities at the San Siro that Friday were impressively respectful. The giant screen opposite the main stand lit up with a picture of the Queen, and Anglo-Italian soprano Carly Paoli stepped up to the microphone. Paoli may be the only person from Mansfield ever to be described by a Pope as having 'the voice of an angel'. She wore a regal red cape and sang 'God Save the King' with gusto. Then she undid her buttons, let the cape fall to reveal her full Italy kit – blue socks, shorts and shirt with a gold number 10 – and she belted out 'Fratelli d'Italia'. Wild applause! Sadly, this turned out to be the most entertaining part of the evening.

England were stodgy and uninspired, and their 0-1 defeat ensured relegation from the top tier of the League. Actually, nobody cares much about the Nations League, but the result (the fifth game in a row without a win) did give fans and media something they enjoy – the chance to attack a man they previously idolised. Slagging off the England manager is a modern variant of the phenomenon Coriolanus mocks in *Coriolanus*: 'With every minute you do change a mind, / And call him noble that was now your hate, / Him vile that was your garland.' While recruits to the British Army were swearing 'true allegiance' to the new head of the nation, the leader of 'the nation made flesh' (Simon Kuper's line about the national football team) knew not to expect that sort of respect.

Three months earlier, England had lost 4-0 to Hungary and Gareth had been booed by fans who taunted him with chants of 'you're getting sacked in the morning'. He was booed again in Milan by travelling fans, and the *Telegraph* reported that the weight of public opinion was turning against him, and many supporters were calling for him to be replaced. Gareth was modestly defiant: 'I think I'm the right person to take the team into the tournament. I think it's more stable that way, without a doubt.' Asked if he was prepared for continuing public animosity, he said: 'Look, nobody is going to enjoy being booed by the supporters at the end of a game, but I understand the job. It is what it is. In the end, I'll ultimately be judged on the tournaments and how we do in the tournaments.' Other England managers had faced similar difficulties but it was his job to take the pressure off his players. 'If it means that the reaction is towards me, that's fine,' he said. 'I'm 52 and I've been through pretty much everything.'

In other words, the deep-seated cultural neuroses swirling around the England team that Gareth seemed to have banished had returned. In fact, they'd never really gone away. Writing in *The Guardian*, Barney Ronay diagnosed the syndrome: 'In many ways Southgate's time has been defined by the unceasing battle with English delusion, English exceptionalism, the self-sabotage of unrealistic English expectation.' Before Gareth, the team was brittle but arrogant.

During his first World Cup he seemed to have solved that problem, but it popped up again in a new guise, Ronay continued: 'By the time Russia 2018 came around, the team was defined by its galvanising, performative humility. We are the humblest. Gaze upon our humility and tremble, for we are England, truly exceptional in our lack of exceptionalism. It worked. The players felt no pressure. The country triumphantly embraced its lack of triumphalism.' The toxic old mindset had adapted to new circumstances: 'The thinking seems to be: because we are now quite good we must as a matter of course be the best. The success of others is an aberration, a departure from some Arthurian state of grace. So the fact England have good players has been translated into "an unstoppable hand of golden talent". The rare success of reaching the Euro 2020 final has become the inexcusable failure of failing to win the final of Euro 2020.'

* * *

Why football fans get so emotional

Identifying with our favorite team can be healthy or dysfunctional. Being part of a fandom provides a sense of community and is related to higher social self-esteem and lower levels of loneliness and alienation.

Team identification is the degree to which a fan views the team as an extension of self-identity.

Highly identified fans feel a strong psychological connection to their team, and a feeling of vicarious achievement when their team wins.

Dysfunctional fans have impaired social functioning, and may engage in behaviors such as confronting others and complaining.

***Psychology Today*, 10 February 2023**

* * *

September 27 is National Day of Forgiveness to encourage us to develop realistic methods for incorporating forgiveness in our lives. Forgiveness is a potent tool on a journey of spiritual, mental, emotional, and physical health …

Forgiveness relieves stress. The stress we feel from anger, resentment, and bitterness lessens and even fades entirely. The burden of these feelings creates anxiety and stress that we no longer have to carry when we forgive.

The act of forgiveness helps us to close a wound. When we forgive, we give ourselves permission to heal. There is freedom in healing.

When we forgive, we also give ourselves permission to stop living in the past. We focus less on the damaging feelings and begin to look forward to the future. When we detach from the heaviness, anger, pain, and resentment, we no longer allow the past to control us. Forgiveness also benefits our physical health. Reduced anxiety and stress mean lower blood pressure, a stronger heart, and an improved immune system. It may also help reduce physical pain.

NationalDayCalendar.com

15
The Shakespearean Hero

20 June 2023

GARY LINEKER was already popular when Arthur Smith and Chris England wrote their hit play about him in 1991. Actually, *An Evening with Gary Lineker* wasn't about him at all. It was a sort of 'Women Are From Venus, Men Are From White Hart Lane' comedic take on relationships, gender stereotypes and betrayal. Three English men and two women (one English, one German) are on holiday in Ibiza. Two of the men mostly just want to watch England playing Germany in the 1990 World Cup while the third dislikes football and is not to be trusted. The two women barely tolerate the idiocy of any of them. The play's jokes stand up well, though the trope about girls not liking football and wanting to talk about emotions and relationships all the time has dated somewhat. But that's not the point. The point is that Lineker is presented as a semi-divine fantasy figure. The main female character dreams of having sex with him; her husband wants him to score too, but only in the sense of goals for Spurs and England. The point is that this mythic version of Gary, jokily elevated to the status of demi-god, helped cement his place in national culture. You didn't even need to have seen the play or its later TV adaptation to get the concept of him as the 'Queen Mother of football', an untouchable icon of goodness.

Could James Graham's play *Dear England* do the same for Gareth Southgate? I suspect it already has. More than a statue or book or even a film, in the land of Shakespeare a prestige stage production does wonders for your place in the national psyche, especially if commissioned by the National Theatre. First performed there in June 2023, *Dear England* later transferred to the Prince Edward in the West End, which is where I first saw it, and has since been shown in cinemas as part of the National Theatre Live programme, where I saw it again. Graham is reportedly reworking his 'examination of both nation and game' for a new run at the National in 2025.

Where *An Evening with Gary Lineker* played mainly for laughs, Graham gave us a reflection on the state of the nation with Gareth as a 'quiet revolutionary' and his team as a metaphor for the new England as they go from perennial underachievers to serious contenders in three major tournaments. The production was fun, too, with uplifting music, moments of broad comedy, evocative clips from old matches, and dazzling stage design. *Dear England* caught the zeitgeist and became a big hit. When I saw it, the audiences reacted like fans watching their team winning a big match.

The action starts in the present, with middle-aged Gareth watching his 25-year-old self missing the decisive penalty against Germany in the semi-final of Euro '96. His unprocessed trauma from that moment drives the play: when he was distraught, no one supported or helped him. Two decades later, Gareth's psychological wound has not healed, but confronting his pain will help make him an agent of change.

When he gets the England job his first priority is to question the culture: why has playing for the national team become miserable? What have we been doing wrong? He brings in psychologist Pippa Grange, bares his soul, and encourages his players to do the same. Gareth understands that their experiences and perception of England and Englishness are not the same as his but are every bit as valid. He and Pippa talk. The team and Pippa talk. The players learn to talk to one another, to Gareth, and eventually to the nation. (Marcus Rashford campaigned for free meals for poor children during the pandemic, forcing Prime Minister Boris Johnson to change course. Raheem Sterling confronted racist detractors and became a hero off the field as well as on.)

In numerous interviews, Graham has explained his vision. In *Esquire*, for example, he noted that the England team was a 'perfectly formed' metaphor for Englishness and 'the health of the nation, psychologically or otherwise'. Moreover, Gareth was a 'Shakespearean' hero. Not a Laurence Olivier sword-waving declaiming type, but 'a gentle, thoughtful, quiet, shy person, who is doing something extraordinary, but what he's doing is really delicate, and how he's doing it is very internal; a lot of it is in his head and in his heart ... Shakespearean protagonists have huge objectives: they want to be King of Scotland; they want to find love; they want to be the richest, most powerful people. What he's doing on a personal level, but also national, is Shakespearean: he's trying to retrieve the Grail and bring it back, and in doing so fix a wound, I think, in the national soul. If he can fix these men, he could fix all Englishmen. But he has to start with these 11 boys.'

Elsewhere, on *The World at One*, Graham said he'd thought of writing about Liz Truss or Theresa May to make sense of 'the chaos and the divisions, and the culture wars' of the years following 2016. Then he hit on the idea of Gareth as 'a public figure who instead of trying to increase divisions is on a long-term mission to unify the nation'. Gareth, he said, was 'asking some pretty difficult questions about our sense of identity, about history, about our past so that he can write with this team a new story for England, and I think England desperately does need a new story in all its forms.'

Graham has been criticised for portraying some of the players, especially Harry Kane, as a bit dim, and he underplays the degree to which the FA was already changing and supportive of Gareth's revolution. There's little in the play about tactics or playing style, but lots about penalties, especially shoot-outs. As the writer explained in *Esquire*: 'The main thing about 2018 was that [England] beat Colombia on penalties, so it was breaking the curse of English football, and it being Southgate who did it ... I went, "There's at least one thing to connect dramatically."'

This approach risked slightly distorting the picture. When Baddiel and Skinner wrote the lyrics to 'Three Lions' before Euro '96, their famous and resonant line about 'thirty years of hurt' didn't refer to penalties because England had only lost one shoot-out, in 1990, and that was considered a great tournament. In the 1970s and 1980s penalties were irrelevant and World Cup defeats (West Germany 1970, Poland 1973, Italy 1976, Argentina 1986) were blamed variously on food poisoning, cheating opponents, bad referees, managers or players' mistakes. Since shoot-outs became an issue in the

1990s, according to the website goal.com, England have been involved in 11, losing seven times and winning four.

Beating Colombia was personally significant for Gareth, but the main thing in 2018 was England reaching the semi-final for the first time in 22 years. And the penalties story didn't begin or end there. Gareth had played in the team that broke England's shoot-out duck back in 1996 (against Spain, four days before the Germany game). And beating Colombia didn't solve the problem permanently. In the next tournament, Gareth's strategy failed (three misses in the final), and in 2022 Kane missed his spot kick against the French.

In other words, penalties became episodic: win some, lose some. And foregrounding them sets up the play's anticlimactic ending. When Kane misses against France, instead of suffering in isolation, his team-mates rally round and give him a hug. Gareth has thus brought emotional intelligence and empathy to the team (and, to a degree, the nation), which is nice but not as dramatically satisfying as properly smashing the 'curse' and bringing home the cup. As so often happens, real life stubbornly refused to give us the happy ending we crave.

* * *

Gareth Southgate has revealed he will refuse to watch a new star-studded play about the England team

Hollywood star Joseph Fiennes has been cast to play Southgate in the play *Dear England* which is about how the country felt in love with the national team again.

But it was clear that Southgate felt a little embarrassed about being part of a stage production at the world famous National Theatre in London and his reign as England boss being put on stage.

When asked about Fiennes playing him, Southgate said: 'That's generous casting! I don't know what to make of it really. The play I think is about the team. No, I won't be going to watch it. It wouldn't feel right.'

***Daily Mirror*, 28 March 2023**

* * *

The head of Russia's Wagner mercenary group has vowed to 'go all the way' to topple Russia's military leadership, hours after the Kremlin accused him of 'armed rebellion'.

Yevgeny Prigozhin said his Wagner fighters had crossed the border from Ukraine into Russia, entering the city of Rostov-on-Don.

Mr Prigozhin said his men would destroy anyone who stood in their way. The local governor urged citizens there to keep calm and stay indoors. Mr Prigozhin claimed that his forces had shot down a Russian military helicopter that 'opened fire on a civilian convoy'. He did not give a location and the assertion could not be immediately verified.

The Wagner Group is a private army of mercenaries that has been fighting alongside the regular Russian army in Ukraine. Tension has been growing between them over how the war has been fought, with Mr Prigozhin launching vocal criticisms of Russia's military leadership in recent months.

On Friday, the 62-year-old mercenary leader accused the military of launching a deadly missile strike on his troops and vowed to punish them. He did not provide evidence. Authorities have denied the strike and demanded he halt his 'illegal actions'. Mr Prigozhin said the 'evil' in Russia's military leadership must be stopped and vowed to 'march for justice'.

BBC News, 24 June 2023

* * *

The disease that could be about to transform football – and cost the sport hundreds of millions

The former Scotland international footballer Gordon McQueen used to tell a story about his time at Manchester United that, in retrospect, takes on a more than poignant edge. He would recall how he once became exasperated by his then manager Dave Sexton, a coach, he reckoned, who was rather inclined to overthink.

Sexton was going through his plan for a corner and after about 10 minutes of complex, choreographed instruction, McQueen stuck his hand up and said: 'Dave, it's a simple game, football. All you need to do is get someone to cross the ball into the box and I'll put my big stupid bonce on it and there's every chance it will go into the net.'

Last week, at the age of 70, McQueen died from complications of vascular dementia. And there is little doubt his condition was exacerbated by spending his working life putting his 'big stupid bonce' in the way of a football. In the immediate aftermath of McQueen's death, the former United manager Sir Alex Ferguson added his substantial voice to a campaign calling for dementia among ex-professional players to be reclassified as an industrial injury.

Ferguson was one of 20 Scottish football figures who issued a plea to the Scottish Parliament to acknowledge that players had been irrevocably damaged by their job, meaning, in the same manner as those found to have been afflicted by dangerous conditions in mining, manufacturing or the chemical industry, they would be entitled to additional state benefits.

Daily Telegraph, 24 June 2023

16
Adelephic Oracle

26 June 2024

DISGRUNTLED ENGLAND fans have just booed Gareth Southgate and thrown plastic beer cups at him. His England played badly in their third Euro 2024 group game, a dull 0-0 draw with Slovenia, in Cologne. The team was as listless and unfocused as in their earlier games against Serbia and Denmark. Indeed, Gareth's men played so poorly, with such a dearth of imagination and energy, that the last ten days may have erased all the happy memories of the previous eight years. Once, it seemed that Gareth had found a permanent cure for the decades-long sickness surrounding the national team. He restored balance and made winning seem routine. In an epoch of craziness, of the delusional self-harm of Brexit, of the fascist post-truth lunacy of Donald Trump, of lethal Covid, of deadly war in Ukraine, of accelerating climate terror, Gareth emerged as the decent, modest, competent leader we never knew we needed. He was England's best manager since Alf Ramsey. Maybe he still is. After all, last night's 0-0 draw with Slovenia means England top their group and move on to the second round. But in these hot, hysteria-inflected days, few fans are willing to notice.

On the social media platform formerly known as Twitter, abuse and mockery of Gareth is relentless. The traditional self-lacerating humour of England fans is back too. Making a joke of fan fickleness, someone has designed a bucket hat that can be turned inside out to declare either 'Football's coming home' or 'Southgate out'. Other wits have pointed out that England could win the tournament without scoring another goal: a series of 0-0 draws and penalty shoot-outs can do the job. Where's the love for 'father of the nation' Gareth Southgate? The man who led England to a Euro final and a World Cup semi. Euro 2024 was supposed to be his crowning achievement. With a truly gifted bunch of players at his command, he was expected to win England its first men's trophy since 1966. But now we see that Gareth love was more like cupboard love. The decades-long sickness around the national team was not cured after all, but merely in remission. The condition that killed the careers of every other England manager has come for him too.

And in a way it was all foretold.

November 2021. Four months after the Euro final, which England narrowly lost at the climax of a thrilling tournament, Gareth is a guest of honour at the London Palladium. Pop diva Adele is performing at her first concert in years, simultaneously launching her new album and kicking off the streaming service ITVX, which my mum calls 'ITV Ten'. *An Audience with Adele* is a glossy throwback to the much-loved studio-bound *Audiences With...* shows of the 1980s and 1990s in which raconteurs such as Peter Ustinov, Kenneth Williams and Victoria Wood wittily fielded questions from invited guests. About halfway through the new show, Adele calls on the beloved England manager to ask a question. Gareth sits near the stage alongside other screen performers best known for roles illustrating Jung's concept of the duality of man. Just in front are Doctor Who and mass murderer Dennis Nilsen, combined in the person of David Tennant. Gangster Stringer Bell and detective John Luther (Idris Elba) are a few feet away, as are mild-mannered teacher/vicious drug lord Walter White (Bryan Cranston), sweet Hermione Granger (Emma Watson) and Cockney psychopath Don Logan (Sir Ben Kingsley). And who's that a few yards to Gareth's left? It couldn't be Jules Winnfield, the ultimate badass from *Pulp Fiction*, could it? Well, yes it could! This moment may never come again: Gareth shares the screen with Samuel L. Jackson, but Gareth is the star.

He graciously accepts the warm applause of the mostly English audience, then banters with Adele. 'It was bloody wonderful watching everything in the summer,' she says. 'It was the best!' Gareth thanks her for her support: 'We saw the videos of you getting quite excited.' This is Gareth being adorably understated. Adele filmed Harry Kane's winning goal in the semi-final against Denmark, but all we could see or hear as she waved the camera about was blurry furniture and happy screaming.

'I hit me head on a cupboard! I nearly passed out!' she explains. Gareth asks his question: 'So, we're supposed to be about collaboration. Sometimes we get that right. Of everybody in here tonight, who would you most like to collaborate with?' She picks actor Daniel Kaluuya, but saucily adds that she's available as a footballer. 'We'll take ya!' smiles Gareth.

The show moves on and soon Adele is singing her signature hit, 'Rolling in the Deep'. The song is usually interpreted as a put-down of an ex-lover. Viewed now, though, at this moment of national anger towards Gareth, it lands differently. On the video, we see him up and dancing along with everyone else. But the song's reproachful words about the kind of tears and despair that follow missed chances should have been taken as a warning.

Tragically, Gareth never even noticed the prophecy.

* * *

Social media risks making people stupid, according to a Church of England report ... The report, overseen by the Bishop of St Edmundsbury and Ipswich, the Right Rev Martin Seeley, said this view of the facts has resulted in the public being 'trigger happy in our amplification, pace and tone of judgement on our individual leaders'.

***Daily Telegraph*, 26 June 2024**

* * *

Serbia did not play well on the field at the European Championship in Germany, but they also had a lot of problems with logistics. The national leadership was silent about this while Serbia was still competing, but now Prime Minister Ana Brnabić has revealed the shameful fact that the Serbian team travelled to Germany on a plane of a Croatian company with Croatian markings. To make the shame even greater, the president of the country, Aleksandar Vučić, accompanied the team and even posed for a photo with the soccer players.

'I can assume that it wasn't talked about because they didn't want to upset the footballers as long as they were fighting for Serbia. But it happened and it's a shame. President Vučic was disappointed and very angry. I expect that those responsible for what happened will be revealed,' Brnabić revealed, adding: 'We have our airline "Air Serbia" and we always travel with it. Even when the president goes on long trips, like to China. It always goes with "Air Serbia", it is our pride when we land with the flag on the plane. I don't know why this happened, but we need to find out who is responsible.'

Delo, 26 June 2024

* * *

President Biden's debate performance triggered a meltdown of epic proportions last night, uniting Democrats of all stripes - optimists and bedwetters - in a state of unprecedented panic. On the biggest stage in politics - with rules and a date specifically requested by the Biden campaign - Biden amplified voters' gravest fears. ...

Biden's obvious frailty, rambling answers and constant gaffes led *NY Times* columnist Nick Kristof to declare: 'I hope he reviews his debate performance Thursday evening and withdraws from the race, throwing the choice of a Democratic nominee to the convention in August.' *The Times*' Tom Friedman, one of Biden's favorite columnists, wrote that the debate made him weep: 'Joe Biden, a good man and a good president, has no business running for re-election.' The headline: 'He Must Bow Out of the Race.'

Axios, 28 June 2024

17
Redemptions

6 July 2024

I SAW Stanley Matthews play. Dad had a season ticket at Arsenal and took me along when I was too young to understand the football. What I liked was the colour of the shirts, and the police band at half-time, and the way players appeared not much bigger than my little finger because they were so far away. Dad often talked about Stanley Matthews. Stanley Matthews was the best player in the world. Dad even took Mum to see him, and she wasn't interested in football at all. And at some point in the early 1960s, he took me to see him too. It must have been his last match for Blackpool in October 1961, when I was nearly five. I can picture other things from Highbury around that time. The great winding staircase inside the stand. Peanut sellers. The height of everything and everyone. The crowd moving under cover when it rained. And I sort of almost nearly half-remember Matthews, though I'm probably mixing it up with film I saw later. And I only mention this because, nearly 60 years later, Dad, who understood the game better than me, realised the absolute genius of Bukayo Saka long before I did. He adored him and thought he'd be one of the greats, like Stanley Matthews. Dad is rapidly being proved right.

It's hardly fair to burden a kid, even the joy-bringing 'Star Boy' whose name means 'adds happiness' in Yoruba, with comparisons to one of the most revered figures of the sport. Bukayo is unlikely ever to lay on a hat-trick for someone called Stan Mortensen in a Cup Final, or play until he's 50, or marry a Czech spy, or get carried off a field on the shoulders of Lev Yashin and Ferenc Puskás. But people are making the comparison. A recent goal.com story declared Saka 'well on his way to becoming England's greatest ever winger'. The latter obviously isn't the former reincarnated (though the dates fit: Matthews died in February 2000, Saka was born in September 2001), but they have plenty in common. Fiercely intelligent and dedicated to their craft, they both have worn/wear number 7 and played/play on the right wing for England. Opponents knew their favourite moves but were/are powerless to stop them. Matthews liked to feint left and move right; Saka likes to cut in from the right and shoot with his left.

That's one way in which Bukayo Saka could be said to link to a past not his own. Another, inevitably, flows through Gareth Southgate. The presence of the words 'demon', 'redemption', 'saviour' and 'vindication' in a newspaper headline from 2024 hint at the reason.

Gareth and Bukayo clearly have a bond. Gareth saw his qualities immediately when he took him into the England Under-21s when Bukayo was 18. Later, he picked him for the senior England team and made him one of his key players. In his early years as England manager, Gareth's favourite strikers were Marcus Rashford, Raheem Sterling and Harry Kane. One way or another they all fell away. Rashford and Sterling didn't even make the Euro 2024 squad, while Harry Kane played poorly.

And in their place, growing ever more influential as the tournament progressed, was the prodigy from Arsenal.

So let's go back to that headline. It appeared in the *Evening Standard* on 6 July, just after England reached the Euro 2024 semi-final. The article following this tells an uplifting story of life chances missed and taken. We already know the first part: when he was 25, Gareth Southgate missed the sixth and last penalty in the semi-final shoot-out against Germany in 1996, causing England to lose the match. It was the mistake of his life, and Gareth was haunted by it. The second part we also know: at the age of 19 Bukayo Saka missed the fifth and last penalty in the shoot-out in the Euro final against Italy in 2021, causing England to lose the match. Bukayo was subject to racist abuse, and Gareth supported him and tried to shoulder the blame, though he was criticised for putting the star into so tough a situation at such a tender age. History never repeats itself, but sometimes it rhymes.

Thus, on the evening of 6 July 2024 in Düsseldorf, came the third part of the story, and behind the indigestible quasi-religious language of the headline we sense a happy ending: 'Bukayo Saka banishes penalty demons as redemption for England's saviour offers Gareth Southgate vindication'. Modern football headlines don't usually read like the titles of seventeenth- and eighteenth-century religious tracts, but maybe they should. Imagine the possibilities: 'A Discourse of Coaching Wisdom in the Impetration and Application of Redemption' or 'Heaven Taken by Storm, Shewing the Holy Violence A Defensive Midfielder Is To Put Forth In The Pursuit After Glory'. I hope it catches on.

Anyway, what happened was this. Against Switzerland in the Euro quarter-final, Bukayo Saka exorcised demons twice over. First, he scored a brilliant late equaliser to keep England in the match, then he nervelessly dispatched a perfect penalty to help England win the shoot-out. But were these Bukayo's demons or Gareth's? The truth is that, like the old judge and the young law student in Krzysztof Kieślowski's film *Three Colours: Red*, they were shared. It's one of the great films by one of the great directors and concerns the mysterious interconnectedness of people and events. Kieślowski seems to be telling entirely separate stories until, right at the end, they come together thrillingly. A misanthropic retired judge, not quite all-seeing but all-hearing because he listens to his neighbours' phone calls, is developing a curious bond with a young woman.

Meanwhile a young law student, who bears a strange resemblance to the old man, is in a relationship with a stormy weather forecaster. We begin to notice that the young man's life echoes the life of the old man when he was young. Critics have wondered who the judge might be. He seems to control people, animals, the weather. He seems to know in advance how events will play out. Is he God? A magician? A chess player? A football manager? At the dizzying climax we realise he has corrected the mistake of his life in the life of the younger man. Which leaves us with a question: just who and what is Gareth Southgate? A humble football manager? Chess player? Magician? A god?

Don't pretend you hadn't already thought of him that way.

* * *

Hanley schoolboy 'capped'

The Hanley Schools Athletic Association has been honoured by the selection of their football captain, Stanley Matthews, as England's outside right in the international match with Wales at Bournemouth on 20 April. The boy has richly deserved his success, for he has been the leading light of the Hanley team during the last two seasons.

On Saturday he crowned a splendid season's work by giving a fine exhibition in the England v The Rest match at Kettering, where he scored the opening goal for the England XI.

Although only just 14 years of age, Stanley is quite a 'veteran' in schoolboy football, having played for his school, Wellington Road, for five seasons. His early promise has been fulfilled, and he has the earnest wishes of all that, having represented his country as a boy, he will go on to attain the highest honours in the game.

He is an all-round athlete, being a good sprinter and a very promising batsman and wicket-keeper. This success in athletics is probably due to the fact that he comes of a sporting family, his father being Jack Matthews, the well-known Hanley boxer.

***Staffordshire Sentinel*, 10 April 1929**

* * *

14-year-old Bukayo Saka made his debut for the England under-16 team on 24 August 2016 as a substitute in a 3-1 away win over Romania. England's goalscorers: Appiah, Mola ... and Matthews.

englandfootballonline.com

* * *

'Now we begin': what the papers say after Keir Starmer takes reins as UK prime minister

After Labour's seismic defeat of the Tories, the UK papers' front pages have focused on the work ahead for Keir Starmer amid his post-election glow after the new prime minister vowed to put 'country first, party second' and rebuild Britain 'brick by brick'.

The *Guardian* ran a full-page photo of the Labour leader pointing the way forward while holding hands with his wife, Victoria Starmer, beside a quote headline from his first speech as PM: 'We will fight every day until you believe again'.

The *Mirror* had the couple waving under the '10' on their new residence's front door on Downing Street above the headline 'NOW WE BEGIN'.

The *Daily Telegraph* also ran with a jubilant Starmer and his wife moving past Downing St crowds while pointing above the masthead to Conservative pain with the headline 'Tories need time to lick wounds', and splashing further down on the new health secretary's warning as the Labour team got to work: 'Streeting: NHS is broken'.

The *Daily Mail* also carried a photo of the couple waving outside number 10 while stressing in its lead headline: 'NOW HE HAS TO DELIVER'. And across the top the paper turned to Boris Johnson weighing in with his '10-point plan' to rescue the decimated Tories.

The *Times* led with 'The work of change begins' above Starmer extending his hand forward towards the people, alongside his wife at their new official home.

***The Guardian*, 6 July 2024**

18
Panto

14 July 2024

WEEKS AFTER it was all over, a Dutch friend was still amazed by England. 'You have Kane, and Bellingham, and Foden, and you don't win the Euros?! How is that even possible? Does Gareth Southgate hate football?' Bellingham of Real Madrid and Foden of Manchester City were voted the best players in Spain and England respectively; Kane was Europe's deadliest goalscorer (36 league goals in his first season for Bayern Munich). From across the North Sea, my friend was echoing a common English complaint: with the talent at his disposal, Gareth really should have done better at Euro 2024. On what I still think of as Twitter, the writer and broadcaster Danny Baker was one of Gareth's most withering critics. He called him a 'C grade talent in charge of an A grade squad' and said it was 'England's misfortune to have had this inadequate dullard in charge of this squad of players at this time. We were always better than Southgate. No matter what his mates tell you.' Gary Lineker was scarcely less unkind. Earlier in the tournament he pronounced England's performances 'shit'. And when they lost the final 2-1 to Spain, he said it was 'a victory for attacking football'. It was strange to see the former 'Queen Mother of football' implicitly siding with the opposition, but it reminded me of the great Dutchman Johan Cruyff's gleeful celebration of Spain's victory over the 'anti-football' of Holland in the 2010 World Cup Final. England didn't play dirtily against Spain as Holland did, but their tactics were cautious and they were comfortably beaten.

I tried to defend Gareth's honour to my Dutch friend. I said: 'He doesn't hate football, he loves football. And he's been a moderniser. And he helped England move on from some of their old madness. But he never was and never will be a Cruyffian.' I didn't need to explain what this meant to my friend, but perhaps I need to clarify here.

Via his beloved Barcelona, Cruyff, the original total footballer and coach, didn't just give Spanish football its current identity. He provided the source code for the ideas that underpin much of the best of modern football. It started with him as the key player in the Ajax and Holland teams of the early 1970s. As a coach, he was even more influential. In Italy, the AC Milan of Cruyff-admiring coach Arrigo Sacchi and Dutch Cruyff protégés Ruud Gullit, Marco van Basten and Frank Rijkaard demonstrated the power of front-footed, positional pressing football. The legacy of that team eventually killed off *catenaccio*. And in Spain, Cruyff's Barcelona 'dream team' of the late 1980s and early 1990s, and Pep Guardiola's even better tiki-taka Messi–Xavi–Iniesta side of 2009–11 inspired almost everyone to try to copy them. Since then, everyone understands the value of pressing, hogging possession and playing a positional attacking game.

Some people think Pep invented all this, but Pep has always given his mentor the credit: 'Cruyff built the cathedral; our job is to maintain it.' As Dutch writer Arthur van den Boogaard put it, Cruyff discovered the 'metaphysical solution' to football: play his way with sufficiently good and well-coached players and you'll rarely lose, except to others playing the same way but better.

Of course, there are plenty of ways to play attacking football that are not Cruyffian. Sir Alex Ferguson's great Manchester United teams were never Cruyffian at all, even when J. Cruyff (Johan's son, Jordi) played for them. But when United were outclassed by Pep's Barcelona in Champions League finals, the difference became clear.

Over the last decade, the brilliance of teams like Spain 2008–12 and Pep's Manchester City have made this style of football the new orthodoxy. There are differences of emphasis, of course, but most top English teams (City, Jürgen Klopp's Liverpool, the Arsenal of Mikel Arteta building on the Cruyffian legacy of Arsène Wenger) essentially follow the same principles. So have many of the better national teams of recent times. The Germany that won the 2014 World Cup was quite Cruyffian. Croatia 2018 and Italy 2021, who both beat England, were partly Cruyffian. The Spain team of 2024 was devoutly Cruyffian.

Gareth Southgate's football life has been outside this culture. He never learned to play in a Cruyffian way and cannot coach it. As a former defender, he favours a more cautious, old-fashioned defensive style. And during his eight years in charge, he did well with it, bringing much happiness to the nation. Gareth-ball brought better results in four major tournaments than England had seen in decades.

But most of his best players play or have played at Cruyffian or semi-Cruyffian clubs. Foden, Kane, Bellingham, Saka and the rest grew up with modern pressing attacking football. They're not used to reactive, defensive stuff and aren't good at it. Without key figures from Gareth's earlier teams – most notably Harry Maguire, who might have provided a bridge – England 2024 were caught between two ideas. Gareth's essentially defensive approach meant they didn't concede many goals, and brilliant individuals in the team somehow kept producing goals to win or save matches. Jude Bellingham pulled off his Klaus Fischer-ish bicycle kick against Slovakia. This was followed by Saka's sizzler against the Swiss in the quarter-final, and Ollie Watkins's spectacular spin-and-drill to kill the Dutch in the semi-final. Even the final produced a dazzling moment: Cole Palmer's precise, potent, long-range strike might have beaten a lesser team than Spain.

But there was always a problem: Gareth instinctively pulled in one direction; his players instinctively needed the opposite. And you're never going to win a tournament playing like a pantomime horse.

* * *

Spain and England to face off in Berlin's Nazi-built stadium

An imposing stadium with a dark history will host the European Championship final between Spain and England on Sunday. Built for the 1936 Olympic Games, Berlin's Olympic stadium still bears the scars of World War II and contains relics from its Nazi past. Adolf Hitler was personally involved in the design and construction of the 100,000-seat track-and-field stadium after the Nazis assumed power in 1933, two years after Germany had been awarded the 1936 Games.

France 24, 14 July 2024

* * *

Car bomb targets busy cafe in Somalia's capital, kills at least nine

A car bomb has exploded outside a cafe in Somalia's capital Mogadishu, killing at least nine and injuring several others as patrons were watching the final of the Euro 2024 football tournament on TV, the government said.

The al-Qaeda-linked armed group, al-Shabab, has claimed responsibility for Sunday's deadly attack via an affiliated radio station, saying the bombing targeted a place where security and government workers meet at night.

Mohamed Yusuf, an official from the national security agency, told AFP news agency on Monday that nine people have been killed in the incident, raising the official death toll of five given by the authorities late on Sunday.

'Nine civilians were killed and 20 others wounded in the explosion,' he said. 'There were many people inside the restaurant, most of them youth who were watching the football match … but thanks to God, most of them made their way out safely after using ladders to climb up and jump over the backside perimeter wall,' Yusuf added.

Al Jazeera, 15 July 2024

* * *

Markets start to anticipate a Trump victory

Wall Street opened higher on Monday, following the failed assassination attempt against the Republican candidate. The private prison sector performed particularly well in the stock markets.

The assassination attempt against Donald Trump is also making an impact on investor mood. The event has further reinforced the tycoon's chances of occupying the White House again, which were already significantly high following President Joe Biden's weak performance at the televised debate of June 27. The market is beginning to see a Trump victory at the polls as increasingly likely, and it is anticipating it in two ways: first, in a search for refuge following the shock of the failed assassination and, on the other hand, with a longer-term view that expects a Republican presidency to bring lower taxes, higher tariffs and fewer regulatory controls. A scenario in which small stocks and banking could especially benefit.

On Thursday Trump will be officially proclaimed the Republican candidate at the national convention, and he is going into the event with the polls in his favor. In a note on Friday, before the attack, Goldman Sachs said that reflecting the change in the odds, 'we have received a flood of questions from investors over the past two weeks.' These questions boil down to 'what should investors do if the recent political momentum drags on.'

***El País*, 16 July 2024**

Epilogue

WALTER CRONKITE half-turns away from the camera, puts on his glasses, looks down and reads from a piece of paper. 'From Dallas, Texas, this, the flash, apparently official: "President Kennedy died at one PM [Cronkite takes off his glasses] Central Standard Time."' He looks up at a clock on the wall. 'Two o'clock Eastern Standard Time, some 38 minutes ago.' Plainly stricken but professional, Cronkite puts his glasses on again, pauses, gulps and continues. 'Vice President Lyndon Johnson [cough] has left the hospital in, er, Dallas, but we do not know to where he has proceeded.' Pause. 'Presumably he will be taking the oath of office, shortly, and become the thirty-sixth president of the United States.'

Skip forward 61 years and on Sky Sports News Rob Wotton, wearing glasses and facing the camera directly, also has an announcement to make. Judging by his tone and halting delivery, you'd expect this to be as epochal as the assassination of JFK. 'But let's break away from *everything* right now to bring you some *huge* breaking news at this moment,' says Wotton. 'And it has been confirmed in the last *couple of seconds* that Gareth Southgate, er, will step down as England, er, manager after [we see footage of Gareth walking down the steps of a plane] *defeat* in the Euro 2024 final to Spain. He said he would *go away* and speak to the important people behind the scenes. He has done that, and he. Has. Made! His! Decision! He resigns as England manager. That news just breaking at this moment [footage of Gareth leaving a hotel]. He took over, er, the senior job in *temporary* charge on the *twenty-seventh* of September 2016 and now steps down, er, from that position. We have a *statement* just into us. It reads like this: "As a proud Englishman it has been the honour of my life to play for England and to manage England. It has meant everything to me and I have given it my all, but it's time for change and for a new chapter…"' He proceeds, we know not why, to read the entire statement, which seems to take an age.

As we picture Gareth's England managerial career lying in state in a large, black-draped room at the White House, this seems a good time for random reflections on the significance of his eight-year tenure as England boss (equivalent, I've just noticed, to two US presidential terms). We might need a Warren Commission, too, to head off any nascent conspiracy theories that might be bubbling out there on the dark web. How will history judge Gareth's time in charge of England? In the words of another American journalist, what are they going to say about him? Are they going to say he was a kind man? He was a wise man? He had plans? He had wisdom?

Jason Burt in the *Telegraph* was in no doubt: 'History will be kind to Southgate,' he wrote just before the 2024 final. 'In fact, history will be kinder to him than the criticism he has faced – some of it, frankly, shameful from former players pushing podcasts.' Gareth, he reckoned, had 'made the impossible job possible'. He might not be a Pep Guardiola or a Jürgen Klopp, but he'd been 'a great England manager. Not just because of what he has achieved on the pitch, where of course he will ultimately be judged, but for what he has done off it. That, too, has been crucial in transforming England, England's prospects and the credibility that has been regained in world football.'

In the *New Statesman* Alex Niven, who coined the term 'Southgatism' to describe 'the peculiar national mood his team seemed to both reflect and recreate', declared Gareth 'the quiet Englishman' who gave us 'glimpses of a better – perhaps best – national identity'. Englishness, he said, was hard to pin down, but at moments such as 1966, 1990 and 1996, the national football team succeeded where politicians failed by 'genuinely unifying a large portion of the English nation'.

At the 2018 World Cup the success of the team 'seemed to briefly point the way to a unifying strain of Englishness that was authentic, inclusive and successful, largely because it was so different from the traditionalist clichés which typically dominate discussion of England and its national soul.' It had nothing to do with 'stiff-upper-lip, knowing-one's-place, Last Night of the Proms' and even less with anti-immigrant and racist political nationalism. Rather, it had the 'utopian potential to gesture at a sort of "dream Englishness"'. Six years later, the team became 'a receptacle for possibility rather than pessimism', 'a cue for imagining different, more hopeful and liberated ways of national being'. Niven noted the similarities between Southgate's 'Captain Cautious' approach and Keir Starmer's 'Ming vase' election strategy. 'There is surely something to be said for such comparisons, and there is no doubt that both England's and Labour's strong performances in 2024 have resulted partly from efficiency in dealing with the world as it is rather than as it should be.'

In 2018, poet and writer Musa Okwonga praised England's multicultural team for 'captur[ing] the hearts of even the most sceptical people in the country'. People used to heartbreak with the national team had 'seen something entirely different this summer: a group of players playing to the very edge of their potential, and beyond'. It was a team whose youth and diversity represented modern England. 'In terms of race and background, Southgate's players were as varied as you might find at a convention of YouTubers or on the line-up of the Wireless Festival.' Southgate's team offered a 'compelling and positive glimpse at the future – where disparate groups of people can come together and produce performances that most observers thought beyond them'.

Six years on, Jonathan Freedland in *The Guardian* was on a similar tack: 'Gareth Southgate was the proto-Starmer, offering during the last Euros a study in contrast with the then prime minister, Boris Johnson. Not for nothing does the historian David Olusoga argue that England under Southgate served for eight years as a welcome island of national stability surrounded by roiling political chaos.' (After the Italy final, Olusoga praised Gareth's team as the best of England and Englishness, the opposite of 'the toxic racism and swaggering hyper-nationalism that has for decades accrued around the English game', contaminating our national symbols, leaving millions feeling excluded from the national game, and damaging our reputation abroad.)

Parallels between Gareth and the Labour leader were hard to miss. Indeed, one of the original hopes for this book was that we'd publish just after Gareth and his brilliant players had won the Euros and just before a general election in which Keir Starmer would thump the Tories. Surely, everyone would want to read about that? The best-laid plans…

But didn't Gareth and his teams also divide the nation? There were and are plenty of people who dislike Keir Starmer, and one only had to open Twitter during Euro 2024 to see that Gareth was not universally popular. The hashtag #SouthgateOut trended and rather a lot of people wanted him sacked mid-tournament. One caller to the BBC's phone-in show *606* complained: 'The football was insipid, it was bland, he's tactically inept, and his tactics is as if he's still got that bag on his head from the Pizza Hut advert.' The press was mainly supportive of him, though often critical of his defensive tactics. From some people on the contrarian right there was vitriol. After the final, for example, *Spiked* columnist Mick Hume railed against the 'Southgate-loving soccerati' who failed to acknowledge the 'millions of England fans' who 'hurled metaphorical pints at Southgate for squandering another chance to make history, and fervently hoped we had seen the back of him and his soul-destroying brand of football'.

The degree to which Gareth's legacy may continue to divide opinions could be glimpsed in Simon Kuper and Mehreen Khan's *Heroes & Humans of Football* podcast. Just before the 2024 tournament they posed the question: 'Gareth Southgate: national hero or overhyped mediocrity?' and gave quite different answers. Kuper saw Gareth's many good sides. He was one of the country's most admired leaders, had modernised the England team, achieved impressive results, and helped redefine our sense of Englishness. Moreover, 'he was a good man. I think there's very few people who would deny that.' Khan, by contrast, insisted: 'There is absolutely nothing remarkable about this man.'

They even disagreed about his football. Was it Brexit-flavoured? Kuper thought not. Gareth's teams 'performed a kind of reverse Brexit', learning from Europeans and playing 'cold-headed continental possession football' rather than the traditional old English style. Au contraire, according to Khan. She reckoned Gareth was 'only doing and reflecting what is already happening around him'. He failed to make the best use of his players from top clubs and showed his limitations when, in the biggest games (Croatia 2018 and Italy 2021), his team took an early lead then reverted to an antiquated defensive style, playing deep, inviting pressure and hitting long balls out of defence: 'Just clear it, lads! Clear it! Which is Brexit football.'

The pair even disagreed on Gareth's contribution to anti-racism. Kuper praised him for saying there was a racist tinge to some of the Brexit debate, for strongly supporting Black players and saying 'England is all of us. England is old white guys like me and young Black people like the players in my team.' Khan gave Gareth some credit but didn't think he deserved 'so many flowers for not being a racist'. He'd reflected changes in the country over the last 30 years and stood up as someone with quite a strong moral compass while the country was having a nervous breakdown around culture wars, 'but if I'm going to give the flowers I think it has to be given to the players more so than Southgate'.

I toyed with ending this book on the example of the Warren Commission, the body who investigated the assassination of JFK, even if there were no grassy knolls on any of the pitches Gareth's teams played on. The Commission's members were wise and experienced, they took expert testimony and weighed the evidence. And of course, when they delivered their judgement, no one disagreed with any of it and it was absolutely the end of the matter.

Except that it never has been and judgements and verdicts on Gareth Southgate will continue too. What do I think, ultimately? I think Gareth was a bringer of joy and despair whose wonderful teams played beautiful and lousy football. He failed and succeeded beyond our wildest dreams. He changed us all but left no trace. He'll be easy to replace and we'll not see his like again.

About the author

David Winner has written such classic football books as *Brilliant Orange: The Neurotic Genius of Dutch Football,* which was shortlisted for the William Hill Sports Book of the Year award, and *Those Feet: A Sensual History of English Football.* He also co-wrote a best-selling biography of Dennis Bergkamp, entitled *Stillness and Speed.*

His versatility extends to writing on politics, penning *The Coming of the Greens,* with Jonathon Porritt, and a travel book, *Al Dente: Madness, Beauty and the Food of Rome.*

David lives in London and is working on a sequel to *Brilliant Orange.*